The Resilient Enterprise

Inspiring the Next Game: Strategy Ideas for Forward Looking Leaders

BCG Henderson Institute

The Resilient Enterprise

Thriving amid Uncertainty

Edited by
Martin Reeves and François Candelon

DE GRUYTER

ISBN 978-3-11-074538-2
e-ISBN (PDF) 978-3-11-074551-1
e-ISBN (EPUB) 978-3-11-074557-3
ISSN 2701-8857

Library of Congress Control Number: 2021938646

Bibliographic information published by the Deutsche Nationalbibliothek
The Deutsche Nationalbibliothek lists this publication in the Deutsche Nationalbibliografie;
detailed bibliographic data are available on the Internet at http://dnb.dnb.de.

© 2021 The BCG Henderson Institute
Cover image: sesame/DigitalVision Vectors/Getty Images
Typesetting: Integra Software Services Pvt. Ltd.
Printing and binding: CPI books GmbH, Leck

www.degruyter.com

Acknowledgments

We would like to acknowledge all of the authors whose work appears in this collection: Chris Barrett, Rachel Bergman, Salman Bham, Rodolphe Charme di Carlo, Michael S. Deimler, Sasi Desai, Knut Haanæs, Gerry Hansell, Johann D. Harnoss, Ask Nørgaard Heje, James Hollingsworth, Christian Ketels, Jussi Lehtinen, Simon Levin, Zhenya Lindgardt, Lisanne Püschel, Martin Reeves, Axel Reinaud, David Rhodes, Filippo Scognamiglio, George Stalk, Raj Varadarajan, Kevin Whitaker, and Jules Wurlod.

We would also like to acknowledge the broader BCG Henderson Institute community: our Fellows, Ambassadors, and operations teams over the years, who have all made invaluable contributions to our research; our academic collaborators, who have expanded our horizons of new ideas; and our BCG practice area partners, who have collaborated with us on several of these articles.

https://doi.org/10.1515/9783110745511-202

About the BCG Henderson Institute

The BCG Henderson Institute is the Boston Consulting Group's think tank, dedicated to exploring and developing valuable new insights from business, technology, economics, and science by embracing the powerful technology of ideas. The Institute engages leaders in provocative discussion and experimentation to expand the boundaries of business theory and practice and to translate innovative ideas from within and beyond business.

https://doi.org/10.1515/9783110745511-203

Contents

Part I: **Building Resilience**

Part II: **Developing Ambidexterity**

Part III: Reinventing Businesses

Introduction

The COVID-19 crisis caused massive disruptions to businesses around the world. Supply chains were disrupted, working models changed overnight, and consumer preferences shifted dramatically as the health crisis spread. Even though the possibility of a global pandemic had been well known (especially after warning signs like the SARS and MERS epidemics that ultimately remained local issues), many companies were caught unprepared, putting some in danger of collapse.

However, not all companies were equally affected by the crisis – some emerged in a position of advantage. The gap between the best- and worst-performing companies in many countries and sectors actually widened in 2020 compared to prior years. For example, like most travel companies, Airbnb saw business rapidly decline at the start of the pandemic. But because Airbnb had a much wider diversity of rental options than traditional hotel chains and was able to flex its portfolio quickly, it was better able to capitalize on demand for new kinds of offerings – such as safer vacations at more remote locations – recovering from the shock much more quickly than its peers and becoming the market leader in rentals.

COVID-19's major impact on the winners and losers across industries was no anomaly – an analysis of competitive performance over 25 years shows that the dispersion between the top- and bottom-quartile companies within industries doubles in times of crisis.[1] As a result, crisis performance is a significant part of long-term success: of the companies that outperformed their industry over the last quarter-century, two-thirds did better than peers during crises.

After witnessing first-hand the impact of a severe shock, many business leaders have expressed an intention to rebuild their companies with more resilience. However, there is not yet a well-codified playbook for them to follow. In Part I of this book, "Building Resilience," we address several of the challenges involved, and how leaders can overcome them to build businesses that thrive amid unexpected shocks.

Chapter 1, "Resilience vs. Efficiency: Calibrating the Trade-off," describes the inherent trade-off between building resilience and maximizing efficiency and outlines several strategies to calibrate that trade-off.

Chapter 2, "When Resilience is More Important than Efficiency," shows how the prevailing mindset in business tends toward efficiency rather than resilience, and gives ways to adopt a more balanced approach.

---

1 "Becoming an All-Weather Company: The value of resilience," BCG Henderson Institute (2020).

https://doi.org/10.1515/9783110745511-205

Chapter 3, "Advantage in Adversity," cautions leaders not to be too pessimistic when facing an economic downturn, showing that many companies achieve advantage in adversity.

And Chapter 4, "Die Another Day: What Leaders Can Do About the Shrinking Life Expectancy of Corporations," shows that overall company lifespans have declined amid rising uncertainty, reinforcing the need for resilience.

Though surviving unexpected shocks is necessary for a company to thrive in the long run, it's not sufficient. New offerings are being adopted, matched, and made obsolete faster, and competitive advantage is becoming less durable. Even if a company withstands shocks, doing the same thing over and over will eventually lead to failure.

To build a long-lasting business, leaders also need to master *ambidexterity* – exploiting the current business model while also exploring for the next one at the same time. Part II of this book, "Developing Ambidexterity," addresses this challenge.

Chapter 5, "Tomorrow Never Dies: The Art of Staying on Top," shows that large, public companies are investing less in exploration and, therefore, having a harder time staying on top of their industries.

Chapter 6, "How Vital Companies Think, Act, and Thrive," introduces a method for measuring corporate vitality – the potential to sustain future growth.

Chapter 7, "The 2% Company," identifies the small minority of companies that have excelled at both exploitation and exploration.

And Chapter 8, "Ambidexterity – The Art of Thriving in Complex Environments," shows how leaders can structure their businesses to enable them to balance these objectives.

Reinventing businesses is necessary in all times, but especially after crises, which usually cause permanent changes in consumer behaviors and ways of working. Part III of this book, "Reinventing Businesses," dives deeper on the challenge of reinvention.

Chapter 9, "Business Model Innovation," outlines a framework for reinventing business models.

Chapter 10, "Lessons from Mavericks: Staying Big by Acting Small," argues that established companies can take inspiration from "mavericks" that disrupt from the fringes of their industries.

Chapter 11, "Leaping Before the Platform Burns – The Increasing Necessity of Preemptive Innovation," identifies strategies for preemptive innovation and how to find the next successful model before the current one is exhausted.

Chapter 12, "Postmerger (Integration) Rejuvenation," explores the role of M&A activity in revitalizing businesses.

And Chapter 13, "Walking the Tightrope: Successfully Integrating While Transforming," reveals success factors in integrating an acquisition while also transforming the existing business.

COVID-19 won't be the last shock that businesses face – other unexpected crises are certain to arise in the future. Meanwhile, slow-moving forces like technological acceleration, social instability, and climate change continue to progress, reshaping what it takes for businesses to succeed. The need for resilience and reinvention, in other words, will continue to grow.

Part I: **Building Resilience**

Martin Reeves, Simon Levin, Sasi Desai, and Kevin Whitaker

Chapter 1
Resilience vs. Efficiency: Calibrating the Trade-off

The upheaval of 2020 has shone a light on the value of resilience in business. Resilience can be defined as the capacity of a firm to outperform during a crisis by absorbing stress, recovering critical functionality, and thriving in altered circumstances. Evidence shows that resilience is a key driver of long-run performance:[1] over the past 25 years, firms that outperformed their industry during crises were twice as likely to outperform in the long run. In fact, crisis performance had more than three times the impact on long-term total shareholder return (TSR) as performance during stable periods.

Leaders are now looking to rebuild their firms as all-weather companies that can thrive in any economic environment. This requires investing in capabilities and structures that increase resilience.[2] However, this creates a tricky trade-off: such investments can reduce short-term efficiency, while the benefits of resilience are uncertain and only accrue over the long term. How should leaders think about making this trade-off?

A Difficult Trade-off

The traditional managerial approach to making trade-offs across time is to project benefits and weigh them against costs using discounted cash flow analysis. For example, consider a firm evaluating the merits of diversifying its supplier base to build resilience against a potential disruption to operations at one of its current suppliers. Such an approach would be to project the expected benefits from having redundant suppliers into the future, apply a discount rate to calculate the net present value of those benefits, and weigh that against the costs (such as increased complexity and reduced economies of scale) involved with such a decision. However, such an approach has some important limitations and flaws for assessing trade-offs between efficiency and resilience.

---

1 https://www.bcg.com/publications/2020/how-to-become-an-all-weather-resilient-company
2 https://hbr.org/2020/07/a-guide-to-building-a-more-resilient-business

https://doi.org/10.1515/9783110745511-001

For one, the benefits of resilience may only surface during a crisis; but the frequency, impact, and nature of crises are impossible to predict. Firms today operate in complex, interconnected environments[3] where even small changes in unrelated areas can have ripple effects and manifest into full-fledged shocks that affect the firm. This poses a challenge in quantifying the value of resilience. For example, to forecast the benefits from building new supplier relationships, we would have to know how often shocks will affect existing suppliers and how severe they will be – an impossible task given the growing and changing types of risks in an increasingly interconnected world.

Moreover, an approach that focuses only on the *expected value* of future benefits is limited if it does not account for the possibility of corporate failure. A financial projection might find that on average the benefits of having redundant suppliers are not worth the long-run costs associated with maintaining multiple sub-scale supplier relationships. However, if the company could go bankrupt under some scenarios without the redundancy in its supplier base, the argument about long-run loss of efficiency becomes moot. In this stylized example, not diversifying the supplier base can be analogized to the "Gambler's Ruin"[4] phenomenon – the strategy may have a positive long-run expected value but a near-certain probability of failure. For example, if there is a 90% chance of doubling your investment each year and a 10% chance of going bust, the expected gain is 80% per year – but over a long enough timeframe it becomes nearly 100% certain that you will eventually lose everything.

Finally, this forecasting-based approach to making trade-offs is not well-suited for the path-dependent nature of crisis response. The value of resilience is not limited to the level of sustained operations, resilient firms can also respond to crises opportunistically in ways that also reshape their business landscape. For example, a company that outperforms during a crisis may take advantage of its position to acquire a struggling peer or enter a new market – with long-term benefits. Such opportunities are valuable, but they cannot be easily quantified.

These challenges complicate quantifying the trade-off between efficiency and resilience. This does not mean that models that aim to project the impact of crises or value the benefits of resilience are useless – they can still help leaders understand how different scenarios could impact their firm. But given the uncertainties involved, they are less suitable for calibrating investments in resilience. Instead, today's leaders need a new playbook to make well-calibrated trade-offs between resilience and efficiency.

---

3 https://hbr.org/2016/01/the-biology-of-corporate-survival
4 https://www.jstor.org/stable/1402732?seq=1

Principles to Calibrate the Trade-off

If the traditional approach for calibrating trade-offs between resilience and efficiency is inadequate, how can business leaders make informed decisions? The study of other disciplines, such as complex systems science and biology, reveals some alternative principles and strategies for making trade-offs that can be applied to the challenge.

Satisfice

Under situations of high complexity and uncertainty, finding optimal solutions to problems is sometimes not feasible. A principle that can be used in these situations is satisficing: following the simple heuristic of "good enough." The idea that satisficing can be advantageous in business might surprise some, as it stands in stark contrast to the reigning culture of optimization. However, research has shown that satisficing is not merely expedient in its simplicity, but it also has positive advantages.

Satisficing solutions are generally faster and easier to implement because they are based on simple heuristics. For example, one satisficing strategy to make trade-offs between efficiency and resilience is to *"build enough resilience to survive plausible downside scenarios."* While this does not necessarily yield an optimal outcome, it provides firms with a simple rule of thumb to calibrate trade-offs that can be executed quickly; knowing that the firm cannot survive plausible test scenarios is a clear indicator that the current trade-off is not well-calibrated and more resilience is required. On the other hand, an initiative to find an optimal trade-off point would require extensive data collection and computationally intensive analyses of all future possibilities – a time-consuming exercise that is likely to be outdated before it is complete.

To execute such a satisficing approach effectively, leaders need to test their companies against a range of plausible scenarios, which may be phenomenon-based ("Would our business survive if a global pandemic struck?") or outcome-based ("Would our business survive if revenues declined by 30% for any reason?"). A variation of this approach is to use satisficing to define a feasible option set and to optimize subject to that constraint. Such an approach is currently used by major banks worldwide (enforced by regulators after the 2008 financial crisis). Banks are obligated to meet certain capital requirements at all times and under a range of hypothetical stress scenarios, but they are free to optimize trade-offs subject to those constraints. The relative resilience of banks amid COVID-19 compared to past crises is a testament to the value of such an approach.

Another benefit of satisficing strategies is that they are robust across a greater range of situations than tightly optimized solutions. For example, during COVID-19, governments faced the trade-off between mitigating disease spread and allowing economic activity. Research has shown[5] that a strategy of short, precisely timed lockdowns was the optimal solution to this trade-off with perfect information, but also that this solution was extremely fragile – it became highly ineffective with even small errors in data, analysis, execution, or timing. In contrast, satisficing solutions (such as sustained but less severe social distancing) were much more *robust* in controlling the disease under a wide range of uncertainties.

Learn

Another principle that can be used to make trade-offs across time is to learn from experience.

One learning strategy is to *assess the firm's resilience in past crises*. Crises provide leaders with valuable intelligence by shining a bright light on poorly calibrated trade-offs. Leaders should use every crisis to critically evaluate their company's trade-offs and adjust their approach if needed: Was the firm sufficiently prepared? Which resilience mechanisms worked better or worse than expected? To this end, organizations can institute reflection sessions as part of their planning processes and conduct post-mortems on crisis performance to diagnose what they should do differently. For example, certain East Asian regions such as Taiwan studied the SARS epidemic and used those learnings to recalibrate their pandemic response plans. As a result, they were better prepared when COVID-19 struck.

Another learning strategy is to *understand the distribution of historical shocks*. Of course, historical crises will not cover *all* potential shocks, as evidenced by recent crises that were without precedent. But for threats that *follow power-law[6] distributions*, such as stock market crashes, the likelihood of shocks of unprecedented magnitude can be roughly calibrated, even if specific events cannot be predicted. For example, while individual earthquakes are unforecastable, their distribution of intensity and frequency follows a power law. So regulators can assess the likelihood of an earthquake of a certain magnitude when designing building codes. Similarly, business leaders can calibrate the required level of investment in resilience by using power-law distributions to identify the likelihood of shocks one or

---

5 https://arxiv.org/pdf/2004.02209.pdf
6 https://dash.harvard.edu/bitstream/handle/1/34651705/68262294.pdf

two orders of magnitude greater than those experienced in the recent past. Of course such an analysis should also not be taken as an absolute guarantee – circumstances and distributions can change.

Adapt

Because of constant change in today's business environment, the desired trade-off between efficiency and resilience may change over time. A guiding principle embraced by resilient entities in such environments is *adaptivity*: the ability to rapidly recalibrate trade-offs as needed. Firms should similarly stay alert to changes in their environment to rapidly recalibrate trade-offs. To this end, firms can build optionality into the business, develop reversible response systems, and enhance business agility to become more adaptive.

Maintaining optionality provides firms with a low-cost way to act on new information and quickly recalibrate between resilience and efficiency. For example, cash buffers build resilience in firms because having liquidity is crucial during a crisis. But instead of raising capital preemptively (permanently building a cash buffer) or after a crisis hits (when raising cash may be too slow or no longer possible), firms can choose to keep a revolving line of credit open. This gives firms the option to quickly raise cash (albeit at a cost) when they sense distress, rapidly trading off efficiency in favor of resilience.

Developing reversible response systems allows firms to make temporary changes to their trade-off in response to short term shocks, which can then be reversed. This can help firms avoid becoming locked in to arrangements that may be costly or constraining. For example, for a firm looking to increase short-term resilience during a crisis by reducing personnel costs, furloughing employees, or temporarily reducing pay is preferable to layoffs. The former is a temporary trade-off that can be quickly reversed, while the latter risks leaving the firm under-resourced to capitalize on a rebound, thus hurting long term efficiency.

Finally, *enhancing business agility* can help firms stay nimble and rapidly recalibrate trade-offs between efficiency and resilience in response to changes in the external environment. Firms can build business agility by staying alert to environmental changes, experimenting quickly and economically with products, processes, and business models, and rapidly mobilizing resources to scale winning strategies. In fact, while the measures discussed so far have involved explicit trade-offs between resilience and efficiency, enhancing business agility has the potential to break that trade-off. Accelerating the clock-speed of an organization[7] increases efficiency by helping firms implement desired actions faster, and also increases resilience by reducing the reaction time to adapt to shocks.

Applying the Principles in a Competitive Environment

The strategies above examined how the three principles of *satisfice*, *learn*, and *adapt* can help firms calibrate trade-offs between efficiency and resilience in an isolated setting. However, leaders can also think about these principles from a competitive perspective, where outcomes depend not just on a firm's actions but on competitors' actions as well. Doing so yields additional strategies to help calibrate the trade-offs.

A competitive perspective provides new heuristics. For instance, we have seen that resilience is a strong driver of long-term competitive outperformance. Thus, a *competitive satisficing* strategy, such as *"being more resilient than competitors"* can be a useful heuristic to calibrate the trade-off between resilience and efficiency. Such an approach can ensure that firms have an advantage in case of a shock, in turn making it likely that they will outperform their peers in the long run.

However, calibrating resilience relative to competitors is not a trivial task. Our research has shown that companies have historically taken different approaches to the efficiency vs. resilience trade-off, leading to a wide spread of outcomes (Figure 1.1). This gives firms the chance to *learn* from the approach taken by their peers during past crises: What levers do competitors use to make trade-offs? What do peers who perform well in crises do differently from others? Which strategies have been most effective in a given industry?

Finally, competitors may pursue influencer strategies such as *baiting*, *interfering*, *spoiling*, and *cooperating* to influence trade-offs made by their peers:

- *Baiting strategies:* Certain competitors may decrease their resilience levels to bait competition into similarly trading off resilience in favor of efficiency (e.g., by announcing plans for a large share repurchase program, forcing other companies to follow suit to attract investors).
- *Interference strategies:* On the other hand, competitors may reduce their efficiency to build resilience at the expense of their competitors (e.g., by paying

---

7 https://hbr.org/2011/07/adaptability-the-new-competitive-advantage

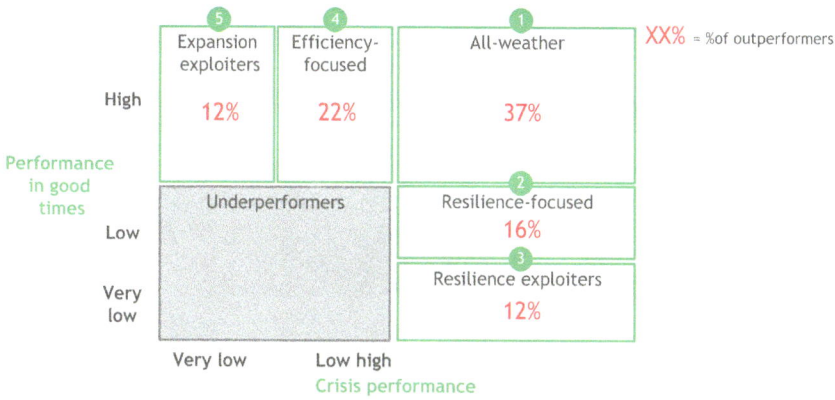

Sources: Capital IQ; BCG Henderson Institute analysis.

Figure 1.1: Companies take different approaches to the efficiency vs. resilience trade-off.

upfront for preferential access to scarce resources from common suppliers during potential shortages).

- *Spoiler strategies:* Some competitors may choose to voluntarily sacrifice both their resilience and efficiency levels if it makes their competition comparatively worse off in both dimensions (e.g., by cutting prices during times of crises, reducing short-term efficiency and buffer to survive the crisis but forcing peers to do the same to remain competitive).
- *Cooperative strategies:* Competitors may come together to share resources, capabilities, and expertise to increase their collective efficiency and/or resilience (e.g., by investing in a joint venture, or by coordinating on crisis response).

Firms must equip themselves to rapidly *adapt* their resilience-efficiency position in response to competitor moves and invest in counterstrategies. Leaders need to stay alert to such moves and devise their own influencer strategies to stay competitive in the long run.

Making trade-offs between resilience and efficiency is challenging, as traditional optimization approaches are not well-suited for the task. But the knotty challenge cannot be avoided – under-investing in efficiency can cause a crippling lack of competitiveness, while under-investing in resilience can cause corporate failure or long-term competitive disadvantage. By adopting alternative principles and strategies, leaders can make more effective trade-offs between resilience and efficiency and position their organizations to win in the long term.

Martin Reeves and Raj Varadarajan

Chapter 2
When Resilience is More Important than Efficiency

The recipe for streamlining an enterprise is familiar: benchmark costs against those of competitors, set cost reduction targets in each area to par (adjusted for scale and scope), and implement. Or, even more simply, set and pursue the cost reduction targets required to increase profitability to desired levels. It seems like a matter of simple arithmetic and an infallible recipe for increasing profitably – but this is not necessarily so.

Take the example of a global airline that was less profitable than its competitors. The reasonable approach, it seemed, was to increase the utilization of each of the most important components of cost – pilots, planes, and flight attendants – thus reducing resource intensity to industry benchmark levels. Benchmarking seemed to reinforce this logic, given that costs for these items indeed exceeded their competitors' costs.

However, closer inspection revealed that the entire system was greatly interconnected. We know that complexity grows as systems become larger and more connected, and that when that happens hidden costs generally soar beyond costs that can be explicitly planned.

In our example, delayed pilots, flight attendants, or planes each had the potential to trigger a chain of delays throughout the system (Figure 2.1). To be prepared to counter these cascades, the airline maintained extra resources (spare planes, reserve pilots and flight attendants, extra gate agents and maintenance staff, spare gates, and so forth). Delay-inducing perturbations were seen as exogenous, uncontrollable factors, and the spare resources were regarded as just a "cost of doing business." Removing the buffers would have reduced planned costs and thereby increased efficiency – but it also would have amplified interdependence and fragility, and ultimately would have made matters worse.

A better solution was to fundamentally reshape the system itself, reducing complexity and interdependence by keeping ensembles of pilots, planes, and flight attendants together. While this seemed, on paper, less efficient than reducing each resource to the optimal level, it led to greater resilience against delays and their ramifications and thus improved overall cost-effectiveness.

The assumption that "optimal is operable" is likely made every day in many industries. It rests on a number of apparently reasonable assumptions that aren't always correct:

https://doi.org/10.1515/9783110745511-002

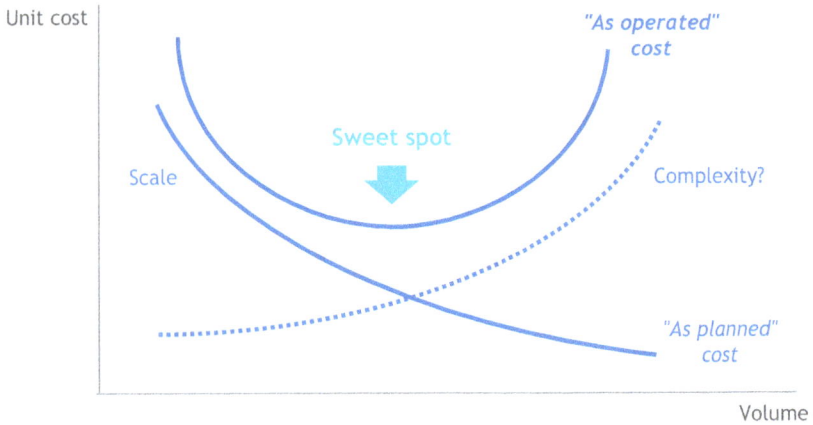

Source: BCG Henderson Institute

Figure 2.1: As systems become larger and more complex, hidden costs may soar.

– The assumption that a system can be understood by looking at its parts.
– The assumption that optimizing parts will result in optimizing the whole.
– The assumption that dynamic behavior of the system is a given, a constraint to be "lived with."

Such oversights are understandable. Financial accounting focuses on cumulative revenues and costs, and there are no standard methods or metrics for measuring resilience or complexity. And the Taylorist approach (the system of "scientific management" developed by Fred W. Taylor) that underpins mainstream management thinking begins by decomposing complex tasks into simpler ones and optimizing and managing each one independently. However, when the number of interconnections is high and when there is volatility in supply or demand, a more dynamic and systemic view of the enterprise is called for. Under these circumstances, the behavior of the overall system is unlikely to be reflected in an analysis of the parts, especially a static analysis. Local perturbations are likely to have unpredictable nonlocal effects.[1] One of the impacts of digitization is that companies have become more interconnected[2] and that fluctuations are transmitted instantaneously, which means that the boundary of the system to be considered needs to be expanded beyond the individual enterprise.

---

1 https://hbr.org/2016/01/the-biology-of-corporate-survival
2 https://www.linkedin.com/pulse/when-everything-connected-else-martin-reeves/

Many managers will be familiar with the idea of systems thinking, but what are the practicalities of implementing a systems perspective to organizational effectiveness? While the behaviors and remedies for each system are unique, a number of common principles can be employed.

1. **Determine if a systems approach is necessary.** A systems approach is less straightforward than a traditional static analysis and should therefore be deployed only where beneficial. If the system comprises many interacting parts and is exposed to a high degree of fluctuation in supply or demand conditions, then a systems approach may be necessary. High fluctuations in stocks or flows or instabilities cascading across the system are also indicative symptoms. The impact will be most severe when a resource with high inertia, such as a physical factory, is exposed to rapid fluctuation. Such situations are often found at digital-physical interfaces. These circumstances clearly apply to our airline example, in which there were fluctuations in resource readiness, a set of resources with high inertia, and avalanches of delays.

2. **Consider dynamic, nonlinear effects.** While the "physics" of a system may look simple and linear, the associated human dynamics may be far from linear, which may force a systems approach. Change management, for example, needs to factor in fluctuating attitudes, cascading beliefs, resistance to change, and other factors. Years of working within a traditional organizational paradigm may build behaviors focused on minimizing costs in a particular silo, regardless of downstream knock-on effects, which are often worse.

3. **Observe the system's behaviors, including human behaviors, and identify the ones that you need to reshape.** For example, you may want to minimize use of the most expensive or least flexible resource, and to do so, you may need to eliminate fluctuations. In our example, the problem was cascading delays and the high (sometimes invisible) cost and difficulty of buffering those delays with expensive resources.

4. **Map and understand the system as a first step in redesigning it.** Create a map to identify inputs, key resources, linkages, and positive and negative feedback loops. In our airline example, flights in and out of one hub were observed in order to understand how delays propagated and how that gave rise to higher use of expensive buffer resources than would be called for in a much simpler model.

5. **Use the map to create a model and see if you can re-create symptomatic behaviors, *qualitatively* and *quantitatively*.** In our example, scheduling different critical resources independently required expensive buffers or resulted in cascading network-wide delays, and the model that was built replicated these outcomes.

6. **Use the model to formulate intervention strategies to modify undesirable behaviors or create new, more desirable ones.** In simple, linear systems, interventions can be as straightforward as specifying a desirable profitability level and adjusting inputs (and/or intermediate operational KPIs) to attain the goal using financial tautologies. Things are not so simple in complex, nonlinear systems, as with our airline example. Often, direct action will have unintended consequences, so counterintuitive solutions – like increasing "planned use" buffers to add flexibility and increase stability – may be necessary. Indirect interventions – such as changing the goals of the agents in the system, aligning beliefs, shaping incentives, or streamlining decision processes – may be more effective than directly manipulating each component. In our example, the key insight was this: adding some flexibility to the system by "suboptimizing" the plan actually decreased the overall "as operated" costs.

7. **Avoid the trap of incremental solutions, which are often either insufficient or hard to design in a complex system.**[3] A clean-sheet redesign of the system will often be necessary. This can be achieved by rebuilding the system from the bottom up, cognizant of the behaviors to be acquired or avoided. In our example, maintaining or increasing buffers was financially unacceptable, so a more fundamental redesign was required. The pivotal insight from modeling was that fluctuations could be reduced by keeping planes, pilots, and flight attendants together and making many simultaneous changes to operating rules.

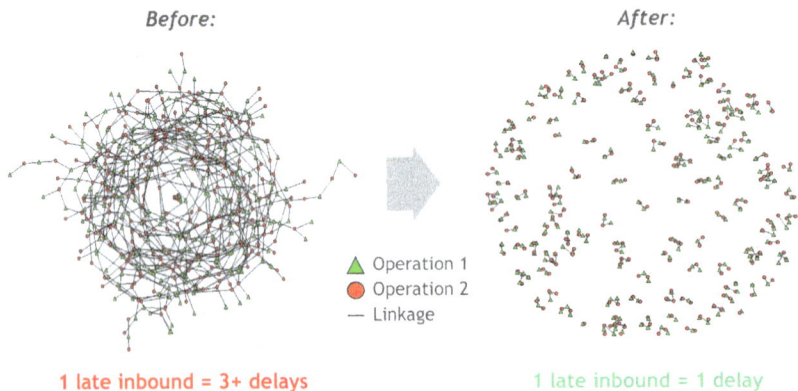

Before: *After:*

△ Operation 1
● Operation 2
— Linkage

1 late inbound = 3+ delays   1 late inbound = 1 delay

Source: BCG Henderson Institute

Figure 2.2: A bottom-up network redesign avoids the trap of incremental solutions.

3 https://hbr.org/2020/01/taming-complexity

The network and the operating rules were redesigned bottom-up around this principle and modeled, resulting in fewer cascading delays (Figure 2.2).

8. **Test solutions experimentally before deploying them system-wide.** While system mapping and modeling will provide some guidance on suitable interventions, the resultant model may not capture the full complexity of the system, especially human behaviors fine-tuned by years of operating in one paradigm. Experimentation will be necessary to test solutions. This is critical because dynamic systems are not susceptible to deductive analysis. Any model is an approximation, and moving directly to implementation could be risky and expensive. In our example, the proposed solution was tested on a subset of the network and, after promising results, rolled out to the whole network.

9. *Measure* and *manage* **for dynamic factors.** Once installed, the new system should not repeat the approach of the past by measuring and managing only period averages and static efficiency. It should also monitor dynamic variables like resilience, complexity, and fluctuation, in order to continuously improve. It is easy in hindsight to deem as myopic the fact that several "key variables" were not measured or tracked. Entities do what is necessary to compete in a context. New paradigms and ideas are required when the context changes. Necessity is the mother of invention, but it can take a long time to snap an organization out of the wrong mental paradigm. The changes required are as much mental as physical.

10. **Don't settle for generic solutions.** Sometimes installing off-the-shelf operating systems, like agile, lean, Six Sigma, or Total Quality Management, can address system dysfunctions, but no system architecture is a panacea: there is no general solution for all dynamic systems. Managers should be suspicious of general solutions to specific challenges. Depending on the context, reducing variance can reduce learning, increasing efficiency can increase instability, or fast iteration can cause complexity and failure. There is no shortcut to looking at the specific details of each situation.

Sometimes the right approach to redesigning an enterprise is a simple, static one but often it isn't, and in those cases a systems approach is needed to reach a solution that addresses dynamic factors like resilience. Such situations, we predict, will arise more and more often as enterprises embrace digital technology and build fast connections with other enterprises. Managers would be well served by mastering the art of applied systems thinking.

Martin Reeves, David Rhodes, Christian Ketels,
and Kevin Whitaker
Chapter 3
Advantage in Adversity

Great [leaders] rejoice in adversity just as brave soldiers triumph in war.
—Lucius Annaeus Seneca

These days, there is often concern about the health of the global economy. It seems prudent for business leaders to prepare for the next downturn – but they should remind themselves that adversity is an opportunity to gain competitive advantage.

Historically, companies have tended to underestimate the urgency, scale, and breadth of responses necessary to cope with and thrive in a downturn. Furthermore, the character and impact of the next downturn will likely be very distinct from prior ones – not only owing to new macroeconomic conditions, but also because the business environment is very different. For leaders seeking to prepare their companies for what is ahead, we offer ten actions to survive and thrive in the next downturn.

The Challenges and Opportunities of Downturns

How do economic downturns affect businesses in aggregate? In studying more than 5,000 US companies across the last five downturns, we found that the average company saw revenue decline by 1% annually during the downturn, compared with 8% annual growth over the three prior years. Similarly, profit margins and total shareholder return (TSR) also declined for the majority of companies.[1] Weaker performance increases companies' exposure to the threat of investor activism – which has risen more than threefold since the last downturn as well as outright failure.

---

[1] Based on analysis of the US economy since 1979 and of US-based public companies with revenue of at least $50 million. Downturns include recessions (periods of negative GDP growth) as well as periods of cumulative decline in annual GDP growth of at least 1 percentage point over two years.

https://doi.org/10.1515/9783110745511-003

Companies' reactions to downturns have often been defensive, delayed, and insufficient. For example, according to a BCG survey of 439 global companies,[2] companies prioritized short-term actions over longer-term initiatives during the downturn of 2007 to 2009. They also tended to act reactively rather than proactively – waiting until their business was directly affected by the downturn before taking mitigating actions – and were reluctant to take bold steps to protect against the downsides or take advantage of the eventual recovery.

But downturns also present opportunities – and to realize them, companies must go beyond a defensive stance.[3] Competitive volatility increases during downturns (for example, the rate at which businesses jump into or fall out of the Fortune 100 each year rises by 50%), reflecting an opportunity to use the downturn to competitive advantage. Investment opportunities, including mergers and acquisitions, generally become cheaper; and some companies use the opportunity to unleash major internal change. For example, American Express was severely threatened in the 2008 financial crisis by rising default rates and falling consumer demand. After cutting costs and divesting noncore businesses to stay viable through the downturn, the company refocused on new partnerships and embraced digital technology. Its stock price has risen by more than 1,000% in the decade since.

The competitive stakes in downturns are high. In the last four downturns, an average of 14% of companies increased both their sales growth rate and EBIT margin despite the challenging circumstances. During the downturns, those companies grew revenue by 14 percentage points more and improved their EBIT margin by 7 points more than the 44% of companies that declined in both metrics (Figure 3.1).

When the next downturn comes, how can your company be one of the few that come out stronger?

How to Take Advantage of the Next Downturn

The impact of the next downturn – and therefore what it takes to win – will naturally vary by industry and company. For example, slowing economic momentum tends to have the strongest impact on industrial goods producers, while consumer goods companies are generally less affected (and often not until later stages, when the downturn hits employment).

---

2 BCG survey "Companies in the Downturn: Expectations, Actions and Preparedness", March 2009,
3 https://www.bcg.com/industries/automotive/resilience-in-an-automotive-downturn

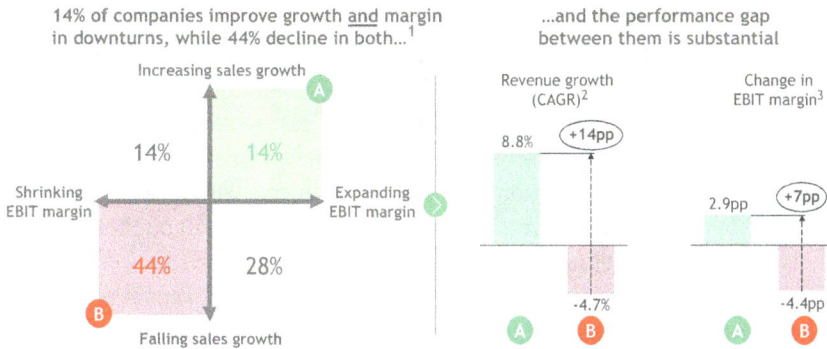

Sources: S&P Compustat and Capital IQ; BCG Henderson Institute.
1. Average across last four US downturns since 1985; based on performance compared to three-year predownturnbaseline for US companies with at least $50 million in sales 2. Annualized revenue growth during the downturn. 3. Compared to three-year average predownturn EBIT margin.

Figure 3.1: 14% of companies increased sales growth and EBIT margin in last four downturns.

However, the evidence reveals some general rules that apply more broadly – giving leaders a starting point to tailor plans for their own companies. Our analysis of impact patterns and success factors in downturns builds on our empirical research on large-scale change,[4] identifying ten ways leaders can take advantage of the next downturn.

1. **Prepare for the *next* downturn, not past ones.** Some advice for weathering downturns is evergreen, but companies need to tailor their strategies to the unique aspects of the current context.

First, the economic environment is different than it was in past downturns. For instance, a small fraction of companies is achieving breakaway valuations and profits. Therefore, there will be more opportunities for offensive moves but also more heterogeneity across firms in their optimal strategies and responses. For many fundamentally healthy companies, the constraint to successfully navigating a downturn may be not cash, but the wisdom to invest it against the right opportunities.

Second, technological change and new competitors are rapidly reshaping industries. This has already caused competitive volatility to rise: though only one in three companies successfully navigates disruptive shifts,[5] those that do often emerge stronger than before. The next economic downturn will likely increase the potential risks and rewards even more – but it will still be only one

---

4 https://www.bcg.com/capabilities/business-transformation/insights

5 https://www.bcg.com/publications/2017/value-creation-strategy-transformation-creating-value-disruption-others-disappear

dimension of disruption among several. Therefore, companies will need to continue pursuing their long-term digital agenda to keep up with the accelerating pace of technology.

Finally, the political and social environment is less stable. With interest rates already low and public debt levels historically high in most major economies – and with polarization causing political gridlock – governments will have less capacity to respond to the next downturn. Increased social scrutiny will put businesses' actions under a stronger microscope. And an economic downturn may further inflame political and social tensions. Therefore, leaders need to ensure that their businesses create social as well as economic value,[6] and play a proactive role in shaping key social and political issues,[7] to keep the game of business going.

2. **Anticipate a wide range of scenarios.** Economic forecasting is known to be very imprecise. The range of realistic scenarios has become especially wide, reflecting several sources of uncertainty that are increasingly affecting the global economy – including trade tensions, political shocks, and the dynamism of complex and interconnected financial markets. In circumstances where many plausible outcomes exist, resilience against a range of scenarios is more important than a single point forecast and plan.

Economic scenarios can be prepared around a baseline projection. Then, for each of those scenarios, determine the specific impacts on your industry and company. Through this exercise, you can stress-test your plans and measure if your company is robust to different outcomes – allowing you to identify the biggest potential risks and create rapid-response options where necessary.

Similarly, because of the unpredictable nature of competition within many industries, scenario-based approaches are also valuable tools to identify and guard against the risk of disruption. The true range of possible outcomes is often wider than you may think. Accordingly, you need to stretch your counterfactual thinking, your ability to envision "what could be" – for example, by using strategy games[8] to widen the scope of competitive scenarios and identify overlooked vulnerabilities. With a wider view of the possibilities, you can assess your exposure to disruption, taking actions to increase resilience as necessary.

3. **Act early.** Many companies may understandably be reluctant to take major actions until they see clear evidence that they are affected by economic headwinds. However, the history of companies' responses to downturns shows that

---

6 https://www.bcg.com/publications/2017/total-societal-impact-new-lens-strategy
7 https://www.bcg.com/publications/2018/case-corporate-statesmanship
8 https://bcghendersoninstitute.com/free-up-your-mind-to-free-up-your-strategy-4bec09783291?
gi=c316320d8dc

the outperformers tend to anticipate the impact and make the first moves, such as reducing their cost base.[9] Companies that wait longer to shore up their businesses are more likely to overcompensate when they are finally forced to act – which puts them in a weaker position to take advantage of the eventual recovery.

Beyond survival-focused defensive actions like cost cutting, companies are also well-advised to act preemptively when making the fundamental changes that will enable them to thrive in the long run. Our research shows that the most important observable success factor in corporate transformation is how early the program was initiated.[10] To recognize threats preemptively, leaders need to pay attention to early warning signals of disruption – whether in the macro economy or from direct or indirect competitors. They need to instill a sense of urgency[11] within their organizations to ensure the necessary actions are taken before major financial or competitive deterioration.

4. **De-average reactions across your portfolio.** In harsh environments that threaten the viability of your business such as an economic downturn, companies need to economize resources by cutting costs and preserving capital in order to survive and grow. But these actions should not necessarily be taken indiscriminately across the business – leaders should also have an eye on renewal, understanding what their future growth engines will be and de-averaging accordingly. In other words, during the downturn, companies should protect the budgets of businesses or locations that still have attractive growth opportunities, while making the necessary cuts elsewhere. In many cases, they will need to both rationalize and reinvest within the same business.

De-averaging your response to a downturn has obvious benefits, yet many companies still find it hard to do in the heat of a crisis. For example, according to BCG's 2009 survey, less than one-third of the companies that reduced costs in some parts of the business also added employees or capacity in another area. To successfully de-average strategy in various parts of the business, you need to develop strategic reactions – for example, by structurally separating business units that require different approaches to strategy and implementation.

5. **Adopt a long-term, competitive perspective.** By threatening short-term performance and survival, downturns present an operational challenge. At the same time, however, they present *competitive* opportunities – which some companies will seize to emerge stronger. All companies must attend to short-term concerns to

---

9 *Collateral Damage Part 6: Underestimating the Crisis* (BCG, 2009).

10 https://www.bcg.com/publications/2018/preemptive-transformation-fix-it-before-it-breaks

11 https://www.bcg.com/publications/2018/creating-urgency-amid-comfort

ensure viability, but those that are also able to focus on the long run have the most success (Figure 3.2).

Perfomance during 2007-2009 downturn by strategic orientation (using NLP)

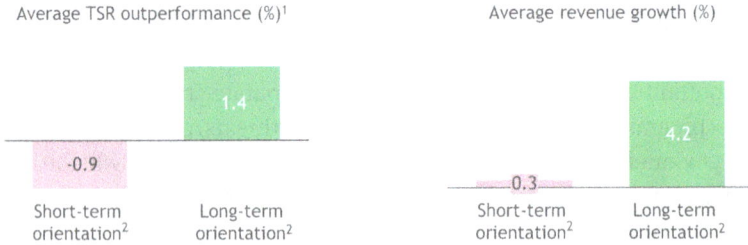

Average TSR outperformance (%)[1]   Average revenue growth (%)

-0.9	1.4		4.2	
Short-term orientation[2]	Long-term orientation[2]	Short-term orientation[2]	-0.3	Long-term orientation[2]

Sources: S&P Capital IQ; SEC 10-K filings; BCG Henderson Institute analysis.
Note: Statistically significant relationship between long-term orientation and TSR and growth (p<0.1) holds when controlling for other factors such as sector and additional strategic orientation scores.1. Annualized TSR compared to average of large companies in same sector during 2007-2009 period 2. Long-term orientation score determined by BHI proprietary natural language processing analysis of management discussion in companies' 10-K SEC filings; long-or short-term orientation based on whether average score during the downturn is above or below average across all large companies.

Figure 3.2: Companies that focus on the long run have more success in downturns.

6. **Use the downturn to accelerate large-scale change.** Even when companies recognize disruptive threats and the need to transform, they often underestimate the full scope of changes that may be necessary. Downturns can shine a spotlight on the long-term viability of a business – which farsighted leaders can leverage to ensure the change effort is sufficiently ambitious. This is indeed likely to pay off in the long run: our research shows that transformation programs with larger investment are more likely to succeed.[12]

For example, Apple released its first iPod in 2001 – the same year the US economy experienced a recession, contributing to a 33% drop in the company's total revenue. Still, Apple continued to transform its product portfolio, investing in innovation and increasing R&D spending by double digits. As a result, the company launched the iTunes music store in 2003 and new iPod models in 2004, sparking an era of high growth.[13]

7. **Invest in growth engines.** Defensive actions may be necessary for some companies to survive the downturn – but to thrive, leaders need to consider the top line. In the last two downturns, the most successful companies did indeed pursue efficiencies, improving their profit margins.[14] But revenue growth was the

---

12 https://sloanreview.mit.edu/article/the-truth-about-corporate-transformation/
13 https://hbr.org/2009/02/seize-advantage-in-a-downturn
14 Companies that achieved 10%+ annualized TSR in the 2001–2002 or 2007–2009 downturn.

largest driver of their performance, accounting for nearly 50% of TSR (twice as much as the impact from cost reductions) (Figure 3.3).

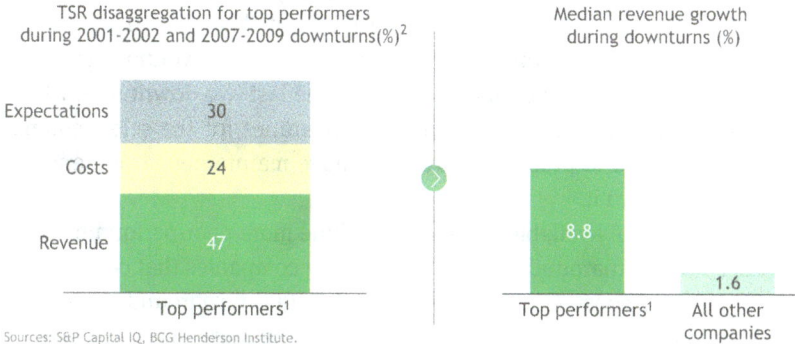

TSR disaggregation for top performers during 2001-2002 and 2007-2009 downturns(%)[2]		Median revenue growth during downturns (%)	
Expectations	30		
Costs	24		
Revenue	47	8.8	1.6
Top performers[1]		Top performers[1]	All other companies

Sources: S&P Capital IQ, BCG Henderson Institute.
1. Top performers are companies with 10%+ annual TSR during a downturn (measured separately for each downturn).
2. Revenue contribution represents average annualized revenue growth during the period; costs represents average annualized EBIT margin growth during the period; and expectations represents average annual TSR above revenue and cost contributions; excludes outliers with more than 100% change in EBIT margin during the period.

Figure 3.3: Revenue growth is the largest driver of company performance in downturns.

Furthermore, growth during a downturn appears to have competitive benefits that continue to pay off: the companies that grew more during downturns also achieved higher post-downturn growth. To successfully grow over the long term, companies need to invest in R&D and innovation, and maintain a balanced "portfolio of bets" across multiple timescales. *A downturn should not undermine the capacity for long-term growth.*

8. **Articulate a compelling investor story.** After revenue growth, the next-largest driver of TSR in recent downturns was investors' expectations – which also had a greater impact than cost reductions. With activist campaigns becoming more frequent and targeting even the largest companies, the risk of not managing investors' expectations is larger than ever. Because downturns on average reduce TSR and profitability – two conditions that increase the threat of activism – leaders will need to make sure they maintain credibility. This involves "thinking like an activist": optimizing financial policies and current performance, while also building strong relationships with major investors and ensuring that the long-term strategy is understood.

Formalized, publicly announced transformation programs are often one component of a compelling story. Internally, such programs can build support for change throughout the organization. But our research also shows that they help build credibility with investors: underperforming companies that announced a formal transformation program were more likely to see a short-run boost in investor expectations, as well as a long-run improvement in financial performance.

9. **Opportunistically pursue M&A.** "The time to buy is when there's blood in the streets," said Baron Rothschild after the Battle of Waterloo. M&A has become a larger part of many companies' strategies, with deal volumes trending upward for several years.[15] Overall activity fell in the last two downturns, which means there will likely be cheaper buying opportunities for the select companies that have the will to pursue it – and that have maintained strong enough cash positions to afford it.

However, the set of available targets will include more poor-performing companies in need of a turnaround, rather than thriving companies that can give the buyer an immediate boost. Our research of nearly 3,000 turnaround M&A deals reveals several important empirical lessons for choosing these deals and making them work. The most successful turnaround deals involved companies of the same sector and with similar cultures, more ambitious synergy targets, and a rapidly initiated turnaround program after the deal closed.[16]

10. **Structure your downturn response across three levels.** To prepare for a downturn, leaders should consider their response across three levels ranging from defensive to offensive moves. The focus necessary on each level may depend on the company's specific situation, but those that come out of a downturn strongest will have addressed all three in their preparation and response (Figure 3.4).

a. **Maintaining Viability.** Downturns present an increased risk of failure, and staying alive is already more challenging[17] for companies of all sizes and in all sectors. Companies need to make sure their business remains viable in the event of a downturn – for example, by reducing inventory and managing receivables and payables more aggressively to protect cash flow; streamlining the core business to increase efficiency and flexibility; and reassessing the long-term viability of businesses – divesting or closing some if necessary.

b. **Building Resilience.** The next downturn is likely to be accompanied by very high uncertainty along a number of dimensions. In order to perform well in unpredictable conditions, leaders must build resilience in their businesses –

---

15 https://www.bcg.com/publications/2018/synergies-take-center-stage-2018-m-and-a-report
16 Companies were considered to have similar cultures if they scored similarly on performance related to environmental, social, and governance (ESG) issues.
17 https://www.bcg.com/publications/2015/strategy-die-another-day-what-leaders-can-do-about-the-shrinking-life-expectancy-of-corporations

Source: BCG Henderson Institute.

Figure 3.4: Downturn response on three levels: survive, perform, thrive.

for example, by keeping financial buffers to be able to respond to unanticipated opportunities or threats; shrinking planning cycles to increase adaptiveness; and hiring talent with a range of backgrounds, laying an inclusive foundation[18] to promote a diversity of ideas.

c. **Increasing Vitality.** "[Defense] should be used only so long as weakness compels, and be abandoned as soon as we are strong enough to pursue a positive object," said military theorist Carl von Clausewitz. The companies that outperform in downturns generally seek growth rather than playing only defense. However, growth is especially difficult to achieve today. Companies need to increase their vitality, the ability to explore new options and grow sustainably in the long run[19] – for example, by assessing competitors' vulnerability and capitalizing on weaknesses by investing in new capacity or M&A; implementing metrics to measure the company's capacity for future growth; and adopting a forward-looking, long-term agenda to win in the 2020s.[20]

The next downturn will test many companies, but it will greatly advantage the few that adopt a strategic approach. By maintaining a long-term strategic perspective, investing selectively, and pursuing transformative change, leaders can help their companies emerge from the next downturn competitively stronger than they entered it.

---

18 https://www.bcg.com/publications/2018/how-diverse-leadership-teams-boost-innovation
19 https://www.bcg.com/publications/2018/global-landscape-of-corporate-vitality
20 https://www.bcg.com/publications/2018/winning-the-20s-leadership-agenda-for-next-decade

Martin Reeves and Lisanne Püschel

Chapter 4
Die Another Day: What Leaders Can Do About the Shrinking Life Expectancy of Corporations

It would be nice to say that I foresaw the future and planned it as it eventually turned out. But at the beginning, for every firm, the overriding question is, Can you survive?
— *Bruce Henderson, memorandum to BCG partners, 1976*

It is well known that business environments are increasingly volatile. They are also increasingly varied: from stable to unpredictable, from fixed to shapeable, from favorable to harsh. And conditions change with increasing speed: businesses move though their lifecycles twice as quickly as they did 30 years ago.[1]

As a consequence, the imperative for companies to match their strategic approach to the specific conditions that they face and to retune it when circumstances change is greater than ever.[2] Failure to do so will result in deteriorating performance and the need to implement risky transformation programs. Such a state of affairs naturally focuses attention on the very short term: on dynamism and unpredictability and how these necessitate agility and adaptation. Equally important, however, are the longer-term consequences for corporations.

We all know the stories of start-ups that overturned long-standing incumbents. To understand how the battle for long-term survival has changed and the implications for both challengers and incumbents, we analyzed patterns of entry, growth, and exit for 35,000 companies publicly listed in the US since 1950 – with surprising results.[3]

---

1 See "BCG Classics Revisited: The Growth Share Matrix," BCG Perspective, June 2014, https://www.bcg.com/publications/2014/growth-share-matrix-bcg-classics-revisited.
2 See Martin Reeves, Knut Haanæs, and Janmejaya Sinha, *Your Strategy Needs a Strategy: How to Choose and Execute the Right Approach*, Harvard Business Review Press, June 2015, https://store.hbr.org/product/your-strategy-needs-a-strategy-how-to-choose-and-execute-the-right-approach/14054?sku=14054E-KND-ENG.
3 We used Compustat's database (1950 to 2013) for our core data set and then matched companies with the S&P Capital IQ database to obtain additional data points. The data set includes foreign companies listed on US exchanges. Analyses were conducted by BHI between September 2014 and February 2015.

https://doi.org/10.1515/9783110745511-004

Contracting Corporate Life Spans

To investigate corporate survival and death, we focused on companies exiting the public-company pool – whether owing to bankruptcy or liquidation, merger or acquisition, or other causes.[4]

While it can be argued that exits constitute creative destruction that benefits the economy, at the level of the individual company they are mostly unintended and associated with managerial failure. This is especially true for publicly traded companies. Some start-ups may be created for the sole purpose of being sold, but once a company has gone public, its primary goal is usually to win on its own.

What we found is that public companies are perishing sooner than ever before. Since 1970, the lifespan of companies, as measured by the length of time that their shares are publicly traded, has significantly decreased. In fact, businesses are now dying at a much younger age than the people who run them. Even though companies' average age at death and humans' life expectancy at birth are not strictly comparable, the opposing direction of the trends is clear. Life expectancy in the US in 2010 was about 80 years, around 10 years older than in the 1960s. This is more than double the average age at death of public companies. The life span of corporations has nearly halved over just three decades (Figures 4.1 and 4.2). Interestingly, most types of businesses in most industries are now dying younger. Only a few make it into their fifties and sixties.

Life expectancy at birth (USA)

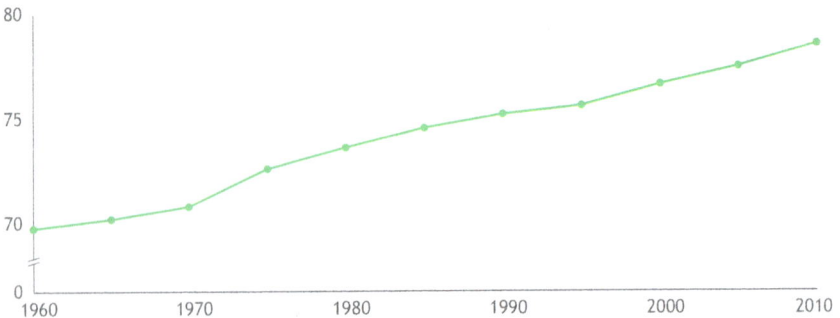

Source: UN, BCG Henderson Institute analysis

Figure 4.1: Life expectancy in the US.

---

4 Exit years correspond either to the database deletion date or to the last recorded instance of income or revenues. Exits occurred between 1965 and 2012, as no exits were recorded by Compustat in the first 15 years of the study.

Companies' average age at death
(for 5-yr periods leading up to year shown)

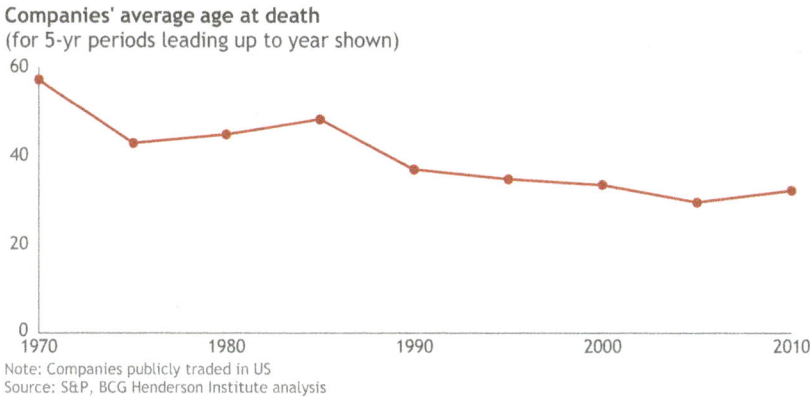

Note: Companies publicly traded in US
Source: S&P, BCG Henderson Institute analysis

Figure 4.2: US companies' average age at death.

So what malady has quietly befallen the corporation?

Rising Mortality Risk

Companies don't just die younger; they are also more likely to perish at any point in time. Today, almost one-tenth of all public companies fail each year, a four-fold increase since 1965.[5] The five-year exit risk for public companies traded in the US now stands at 32 percent, compared with the 5–10 percent risk they would have faced 50 years ago (Figure 4.3).

Why do these statistics matter to leaders? While not every manager will worry about the fate of his or her business 100 years from now, a one-in-three chance of not successfully surviving the next five years falls within typical CEO tenures and investor time horizons – and is therefore relevant to both.[6]

---

5 Research described in a recent paper (Daepp et al., "The Mortality of Companies," *Journal of the Royal Society Interface*, Vol. 12, May 2015) appears to have produced different results. However, it is possible that the authors' distribution-based approach obscured variations in birth and exit rates over time. Given the nature of the data set, we believe that a longitudinal approach allows for more nuanced insights.

6 Leaders around the globe are beginning to catch on to this trend. See, for example, recent remarks by outgoing Cisco CEO, John Chambers (" Retiring CEO delivers dire prediction: 40% of companies will be dead in 10 years," *Business Insider*, June 8, 2015), https://www.businessin sider.com/chambers-40-of-companies-are-dying-2015-6.

Average 5-yr exit risk by sector
5-yr moving average[1]

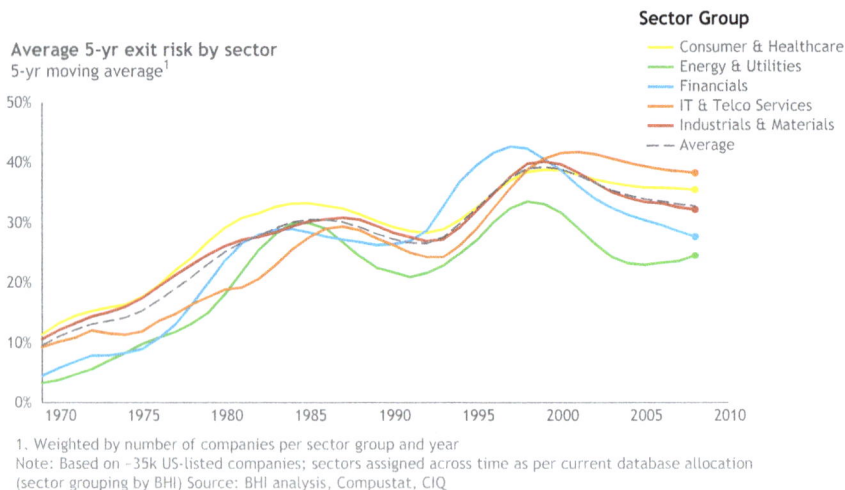

1. Weighted by number of companies per sector group and year
Note: Based on ~35k US-listed companies; sectors assigned across time as per current database allocation
(sector grouping by BHI) Source: BHI analysis, Compustat, CIQ

Figure 4.3: Five-year exit risk of US companies by sector.

One might expect particular types of companies, such as new entrants in the technology sector, to account for most of the observed shift. Surprisingly, however, our research shows that the surge in mortality risk is widespread:

- *There are no safe harbors.* Mortality risk grew relatively uniformly across all sectors of the economy. Only the past decade saw a slight divergence in outcomes: traditionally stable oligopolies (such as the oil and gas industry) recovered the most, while mortality remains high in more dynamic industries (such as technology).

- *Neither scale nor experience is a safeguard.* Mortality risk also grew for companies of all sizes and ages. While smaller companies have always faced greater risk, even the largest companies are now facing higher exit rates. Company age only began to affect exit risk in the first decade of the 2000s, when turnover plateaued for older companies but continued to grow among younger ones.

What is Driving the Mortality Trend?

We believe that a dynamic not unlike the succession sequence in forests and other ecosystems has been unfolding and driving these trends:

- In the economic and venture-capital-funding booms of the mid-1980s and mid- to late-'90s, many smaller and younger companies entered the public markets.
- These companies had a more than 25 percent higher risk of failure compared with the average company – likely owing to poorer quality (a lower bar for entry), few buffers against failure (lack of resources), and intense peer pressure (the smallest companies faced the highest competitive density).[7]
- Those that endured grew into serious competitors for incumbents, driving up the death rate among medium-size and large established companies, which were often unable to react quickly enough to the disruptions wrought by these smaller upstarts.
- Surviving incumbents then began to react by acquiring small- to medium-size companies, again driving up exit rates in this segment while stabilizing turnover among large companies.

Take the example of Compaq Computer. Founded in 1982, it went public and shot to success extremely quickly. Unlike many of its peers (Altos Computer Systems, Corona Data Systems, Eagle Computer, and Osborne Computer), Compaq survived into the '90s, establishing itself as a serious threat to incumbents in the computer industry. Among the much older and larger incumbents it disrupted was DEC, which was sold to Compaq in 1998. Another giant, HP, saved itself from the same fate by buying up Compaq after the company struggled through the dot-com collapse.

A Growth-Endurance Trade-Off?

We observed a surprising relationship between revenue growth and mortality: while the fastest-shrinking companies are most likely to perish, they are closely followed by the fastest growers.[8] That is, accelerated growth correlates with shorter lifespans, whereas companies with more moderate growth face the lowest risk.

In theory, decreasing lifespans coupled with such a growth-exit relationship could merely indicate an acceleration in the corporate value-generation cycle. That is, companies might simply be achieving their full potential in less time.

---

7 These companies were less than 10 years old and had less than $50 million in sales. During peak mortality periods for this group, more than 50 percent of market entries were small companies.

8 This correlation holds true across the entire period of analysis and remains significant even when controlling for factors such as age, size, industry, and profitability.

A closer look at the data, however, reveals that the contraction of corporate lifespans, on average, diminishes long-term value creation. Over the period of our analysis, the average cumulative profits of public companies declined at an even sharper rate than corporate lifespans. Across cohorts, companies that died younger tended to generate lower lifetime EBIT. Longer-lived companies thus appear to create more value than fast-growing, short-lived ones.

Attaining Sustainable Long-Term Performance

Shorter lifespans and diminished lifetime value constitute a strong trend – but not an inevitability. The same can be said about the relationship between growth and mortality. While it is ever tougher for companies to sustain viability and performance, there is also a broader spread of outcomes – and there are examples of companies that manage to successfully endure (such as Procter & Gamble, Johnson & Johnson, Coca-Cola, and Disney).

Many CEOs intuitively sense the challenge of accelerated mortality. Not long ago, for example, one of Asia's emerging global-challenger companies asked us what governance arrangements would best ensure its survival and prosperity for the next 100 years.

So what can corporations do now to strengthen their long-term resilience without undermining performance? We have a number of suggestions based on our own research and the work of others on systems resilience.

1. **Detect early-warning signals.** The bare-minimum condition that will enable a company to adjust to changing circumstances is an external orientation and an awareness of change signals and their significance. The dominant logic that sustains success in slow-moving environments can easily become a mental filter preventing corporations from seeing threats to their viability. Similarly, when a company focuses on rapid change in a volatile environment, it can easily miss more slowly unfolding signals that indicate vulnerability in the longer term. Such an external orientation is as much about mind-set as it is about acquiring crucial information before it is too late.

2. **Adapt your strategy to your environment.** Imperative to safeguarding the future is surviving the present. Today's great variety of business environments means that the same approach will not work everywhere; for example, the planning routines of classical strategy will not work in dynamic and unpredictable industries. Our research confirms that companies that match their

strategic approach to their specific environment survive with the highest total lifetime value.[9]

3. **Run and reinvent.** Environments are not only more diverse, they are also more dynamic than they were in the past, meaning that circumstances change much more rapidly and unpredictably. It is therefore essential not only to get the match right between the situation and the approach to strategy and execution, but also to ensure that the company can regularly retune itself to changing situations. Most companies today need to both run and reinvent themselves continuously, in each part of their business.[10]

4. **Aim for resilience on all time scales.** While immediate business risks should not go unaddressed, increasing dynamism across industries may have caused many companies to adopt an excessively short-term focus. This is reflected in the recent emphasis on achieving agility and adaptability, as well as in the growing tendency to assess leaders in terms of annual or even quarterly performance. While all these measures promote short-term survival, they can also lead to the neglect of longer-term horizons. Our research shows that companies need to be resilient on all time scales. Put another way, they need to be able to sustain their adaptiveness in order to avoid becoming "disposable" corporations.

5. **But don't confuse persistence with performance.** While company lifespan is an indicator of total lifetime value, simply enduring does not guarantee increased value creation. If a company cannot achieve sustained performance, it shouldn't persist just for the sake of it. A successful exit may be better than languishing and slowly burning up resources.

Renew Your Governance Model

How can leaders ensure resilience well beyond their own tenures in the face of circumstances that cannot be anticipated? In the longer term, the key lies in building the right sort of governance model. This means setting up the company's

---

9 Based on the BCG Henderson Institute's multiarmed-bandit simulation; we included a mortality condition and examined lifetime profits. See Reeves et al., Your Strategy Needs a Strategy, https://store.hbr.org/product/your-strategy-needs-a-strategy-how-to-choose-and-execute-the-right-approach/14054?sku=14054E-KND-ENG.

10 See Martin Reeves, "Algorithms Can Make Your Organization Self-Tuning," *Harvard Business Review*, May 13, 2015, https://hbr.org/2015/05/algorithms-can-make-your-organization-self-tuning.

board structure and decision mechanisms with a view to endurance. We have identified four key governance principles that promote longevity:

1. *Cohesion.* Avoid implosion. Align internal and external stakeholders around a clear and common mission and pay attention to succession planning.
2. *Prudence.* Avoid overextension and vulnerability to infrequent but severe risks. Create a modular structure with buffers to prevent the escalation of shocks; focus on long-term health, not immediate TSR; and stress test your plans against 10- or even 100-year risk events.
3. *Adaptiveness.* Avoid being made obsolete by change. Implement a culture of information gathering, experimentation, selection, and iteration; strive to harness a diversity of perspectives.
4. *Embeddedness.* Avoid becoming an object of external (legal or social) sanction. Foster transparency, connectivity, and co-evolution with your company's social, cultural, and natural environment. Bake sustainability principles into your business planning.

Against an increased risk of accelerated mortality, leaders who think on multiple time scales – and make sure that their organizations do, too – can defy the odds and ensure longevity and prosperity for their enterprises.

Part II: **Developing Ambidexterity**

Martin Reeves, Knut Haanæs, and Johann D. Harnoss

Chapter 5
Tomorrow Never Dies: The Art of Staying on Top

Shining today, gone tomorrow? For every Apple, there is an Atari, for every Fuji a Polaroid, and for every Netflix a Blockbuster. It's harder to stay on top than to get there. How can you avoid the seemingly inevitable and become an "evergreen" corporation?

In the last chapter, we showed that companies die sooner than ever before: one in three public companies overall and one in six large companies will not survive the next five years (Figure 4.3). We now reveal that despite this threat to their longevity, companies are more focused than ever on the short term. This failure to take the long view is often a result of past success – a phenomenon we call the "success trap."

The biggest threat to the survival of large companies may therefore come not from Silicon Valley or China, but from their own lack of strategic renewal. The good news is that premature demise is far from inevitable. Leaders hold their companies' fates in their hands. We offer five action imperatives to help leaders turn their companies into sustainably growing, value-creating, evergreen corporations.

Large, Established Companies are Increasingly Vulnerable

In the 1960s, BCG's founder, Bruce Henderson, said that bigness is a big idea. High relative market share yields lower costs, which generate more cash to fund growth, creating a virtuous cycle of sustained competitive advantage. But size no longer means what it used to: today, only 7% of companies that are market share leaders are also profit leaders in their industries – down from 25% in the 1960s. Scale is thus increasingly an indication of past success, not a predictor of future performance.

Scale can also deceive: it initially serves as a buffer against external pressures, making large, established companies generally more resilient than smaller, younger ones. This resilience, however, does not compensate indefinitely for insufficient investments in future growth options. Size frequently leads to inertia, slowly driving up mortality even among the largest companies.

https://doi.org/10.1515/9783110745511-005

Embracing the Dynamism and Diversity of Business Environments

Large companies cannot afford to be complacent. Markets are more dynamic than in the past, requiring companies to innovate and self-disrupt more frequently and decisively. Market conditions are also more diverse than ever before, so companies must tailor their approaches to strategy and execution[1] in order to suit these various environments. Large companies comprising multiple businesses need to develop a tailored approach simultaneously for each part of their business and revisit the resulting collage of approaches as circumstances change. That requires them to be ambidextrous: to apply different and even contradictory approaches to strategy and execution in different parts of their business. It is a difficult feat, but indispensable: our research shows that while only a small minority of companies achieve ambidexterity, those that do perform significantly better than those that do not.

Ambidexterity also means balance – exploiting existing business options while exploring new ones, running and reinventing the company at the same time. Exploratory activities include searching for, nurturing, and scaling growth opportunities, whereas exploitative activities involve refining existing recipes for success. Big corporations with a legacy of success in their core businesses often tend toward overexploitation. They overestimate the longevity of their products and business models and underinvest in building new ones. Ironically, when results begin to fade, these companies often respond by setting off a vicious cycle of cost reductions and share buybacks. Such interventions tend to further marginalize exploratory activities and lead the company onto an inexorable path toward the success trap.

What is this trap, and why do companies fall into it?

Meet the Success Trap

To answer those questions, we measured the degree of exploration in the S&P 500 by calculating the present value of growth options (PVGO)[2] of each listed company.

---

[1] See Martin Reeves, Knut Haanaes, and Janmejaya Sinha, *Your Strategy Needs a Strategy: How to Choose and Execute the Right Approach* (Boston: Harvard Business Review Press, 2015), https://store.hbr.org/product/your-strategy-needs-a-strategy-how-to-choose-and-execute-the-right-approach/14054?sku=14054E-KND-ENG.

[2] The present value of growth options (PVGO) is based on a methodology developed in Han T.J. Smit and Lenos Trigeorgis, *Strategic Investment: Real Options and Games* (Princeton:

Our findings are striking: public US companies struggle to keep exploring. In the past ten years, the degree of exploration (PVGO in relation to market capitalization) for the S&P 500 as a whole decreased by 7 percentage points. The 125 largest S&P 500 companies saw an even steeper decline – of 10 percentage points (Figure 5.1). This movement is broad based – only one in four large companies bucks the trend – and it represents an enormous decline in future options value. Investors now value the future growth of these large companies at a staggering $1 trillion less than they did a decade ago. This implies that the stock market rally that began in 2009 was fueled predominantly by higher current earnings, dividends, and share buybacks rather than by the creation of future growth options.

Present value of future growth options (PVGO)
as a % of market capitalization

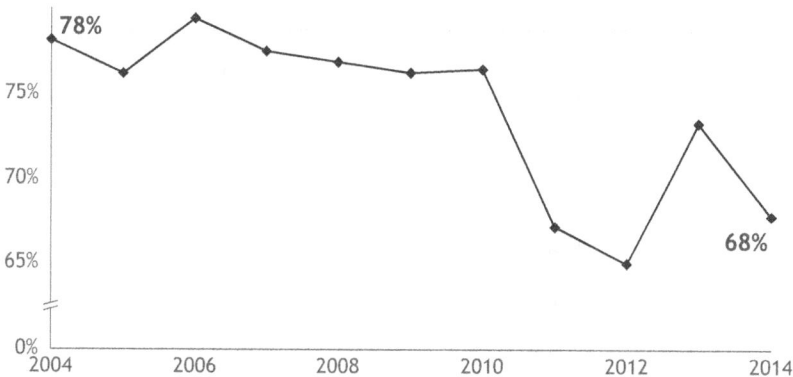

Note: Constant 2004 cohort of largest 125 companies in S&P 500
Source: BCG Henderson Institute analysis

Figure 5.1: The 125 largest S&P 500 companies saw a 10 percent decline in present value of growth options.

A large portion of the decline in exploration is accounted for by companies that have been S&P 500 members for a long time. Those companies are often strategically and organizationally locked into their historically successful business models. As a result, they are less exploratory – by close to 20 percentage

Princeton University Press, 2004). PVGO is calculated as the residual from a company's market capitalization and the perpetuity of its current dividend stream (taking into account firm-specific beta, yearly US risk-free rates, and an equity market premium derived from investor surveys) and expressed as a proportion of the company's market capitalization. We consider PVGO to be a useful proxy for the true extent of exploration activities but by no means an exhaustive measure. A more granular assessment requires internal company data.

points – than their younger peers. These established companies have also seen the most dramatic reductions in their exploratory activity. As a result, the trend away from exploration toward exploitation is driven overwhelmingly by large and by established companies.[3]

To be clear, the turn toward exploitation may not immediately affect investors, because companies can maintain earnings and shareholder returns in the short term by cutting costs, increasing dividends, and pursuing share buybacks. Such companies become "value stocks" – essentially bonds, in the eyes of investors – and are stuck on a path of low growth and continual efficiency improvements, which are hard to sustain. This path leads to a trap of overexploitation – the success trap.

Our research shows that companies in this trap significantly underperform in the long term relative to[4] the companies at the other end of the spectrum (Figure 5.2). Over a ten-year period, explorers grew faster than exploiters (their annual sales growth was nearly 6 percentage points higher) and delivered higher long-term total shareholder returns (by 2.4 percentage points per year). Those patterns also fully apply within industries – exploratory companies outperform their exploitative industry peers on both dimensions.

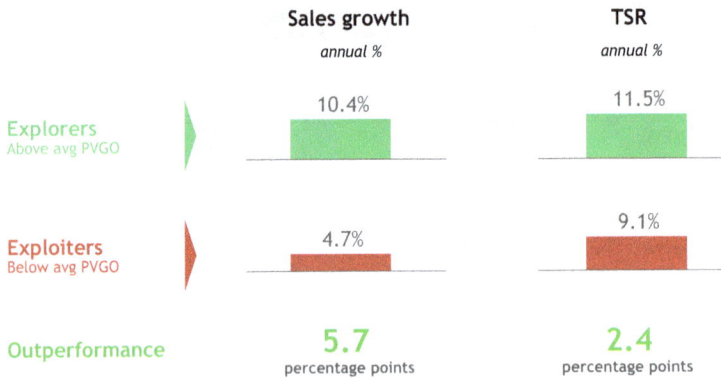

Note: Based on 2004 PVGO and 2004-14 performance
Source: BCG Henderson Institute analysis

Figure 5.2: Over a ten-year period, explorers grew faster than exploiters and delivered higher long-term total shareholder returns.

---

3 We weight S&P 500 companies equally. Our results for the S&P 500 companies are thus not directly driven by firm size or value.
4 We define explorers as firms with PVGO as a % of market capitalization above the median of the S&P 500 peer group and exploiters as firms below the median.

Fortunately, not all companies fall into the success trap. Young companies have to balance exploration (developing winning products and business models) and exploitation (generating cash to support growth) in order to survive and thrive. Some companies maintain this dual discipline even when they attain scale. Amazon and Google, for example, are able to sustain their exploratory drive while focusing on operational efficiency and commercial excellence.

Only one in ten companies manages to follow this example. The remaining nine do not stay in the top right quadrant over a ten-year period. These companies, often formerly successful, follow a predictable path toward overexploitation – overoptimizing and overrelying on their past recipes for success. Over a five-year period, three of those nine companies keep following the path and end up falling into the success trap (Figure 5.3).

Value of growth options as % of share price, 2014

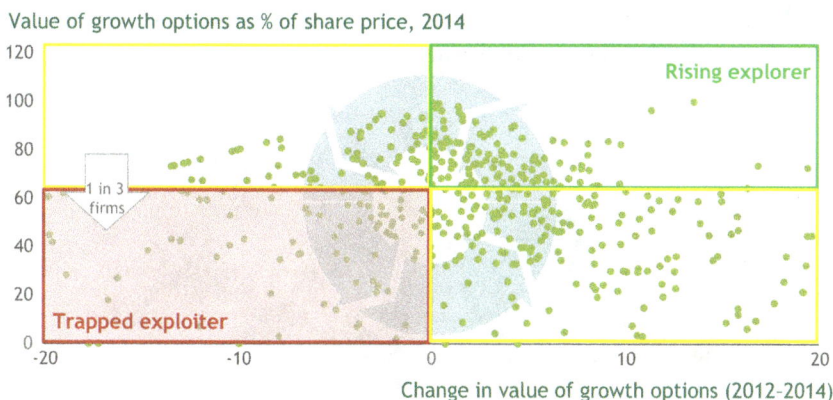

Note: Based on S&P500 US companies, 2004-2014.
Source: BCG Henderson Institute analysis

Figure 5.3: Over a five-year period, one in three companies following the overexploitation path and end up falling into the success trap.

Paradoxically, doing so often seems like the right choice. Fine-tuning the current, successful model provides higher immediate rewards at low risk for the company and its managers and shareholders. But this choice comes at the cost of lower growth, which jeopardizes the company's future. Fast-forward a few years, and lower growth means fewer interactions with new, demanding customer groups and less inspiration to innovate. Eventually, the company is likely to be out of touch with changing market requirements. At that point, it is often too late to correct course. The company has fallen into the success trap. Our research shows that it is surprisingly difficult to escape this trap. More than two in three companies fail to get back onto the path of exploration within five years.

Five Imperatives for Action

Big companies need to avoid the success trap if they aspire to become evergreen corporations. Executives can steer their companies away from the trap by executing the right approaches to strategy for each part of the business, cultivating the right capabilities, organizing appropriately, and leading in the right manner.

1. **Adopt the right approach to strategy and execution in each part of the business.** Your strategy needs a strategy.[5] In other words, leaders need to extend their repertoire beyond analysis, prediction, and planning. This classical approach to strategy may work when the environment is highly predictable; but less predictable, more malleable, or even harsh conditions call for other approaches (Figure 5.4). Developing these new approaches is easier said than done. In order to execute effective strategies for such business environments, companies need to build new adaptive and shaping capabilities.

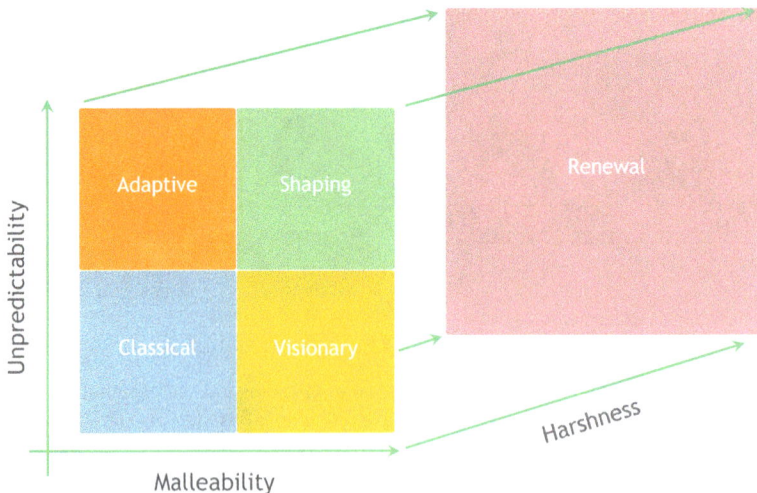

Source: BCG Henderson Institute

Figure 5.4: Leaders need to extend their repertoire beyond classical strategy.

2. **Cultivate an adaptive capability.** Unpredictable environments require rapid adjustment to changing market conditions. Young companies understand this intuitively, moving through "vary, select, and amplify" cycles until they find a successful model to scale. To some extent, big companies need to unlearn their

5 https://www.bcg.com/publications/collections/your-strategy-needs-strategy/intro

predisposition toward planning, prediction, and precision and relearn how to pursue disciplined experimentation. Tata Consultancy Services, an IT service provider, is an example of a large company that executes such an adaptive approach to strategy by encouraging experimentation.

3. **Cultivate a shaping capability.** Scale may not guarantee sustained success, but it can help a company shape its environment by deploying influence in a wider ecosystem. Apple, for example, forged its initial groundbreaking deals with the five major record labels in 2002 thanks to its large user base and the music industry's trust in Apple's technology competence. Leaders of large companies need to recognize their potential influence and use it to shape business ecosystems.

4. **Cultivate ambidexterity.** Choosing the right approaches to strategy and execution is not enough. Big companies need to continually adjust the balance of strategic approaches across their businesses in order to simultaneously run and reinvent the company. Metrics and incentives for continual exploration can help. 3M, for example, pioneered the New Product Vitality Index (NPVI), a metric that tracks the share of sales from products that didn't exist five years ago. But companies need to go beyond introducing one new metric. Corporate centers should consider de-averaging performance contracts across business units and employing differentiated steering models. Pfizer provides a case in point. The pharma company takes different strategic approaches and cultivates different cultures in its global innovative pharma and global established pharma units.

Such variety can be hard to contain under the same roof. Hence, companies need to adapt the structure of the organization to safeguard exploration and maintain ambidexterity. An example is Google's reorganization into Alphabet, which separated the more mature search business from exploratory units such as Google X. A more radical approach is to split the company, as eBay did with the spin-off of its PayPal business.

In more dynamic environments, businesses should consider self-organization. Alibaba, the Chinese e-commerce giant, employs self-steering teams to continually match its business to market conditions through co-creation sessions with customers. Through this process, the company has morphed itself from an export marketplace into an evolving portfolio of e-commerce-related businesses – and has solidified its position as China's most valuable tech company.

5. **Animate the resulting collage of strategy approaches.** A company's journey to become an ambidextrous organization starts and ends with its leaders. To animate the collage of strategy approaches and overcome the organization's

natural tendency to rely on familiar, comfortable, or formerly successful recipes, leaders must reconceive their role. In particular, they need to cultivate a state of artful disequilibrium throughout the organization. To amplify their efforts, they must build a leadership team that is committed to the health of the overall portfolio, not to the championing and protection of individual businesses. Above all, leaders need their teams to embrace the contradictory requirements of exploration and exploitation. As Peter Hancock, the CEO of AIG, told us, "I always hear, 'You're giving me mixed messages.' I say, 'You're a leader – you're paid to deliver mixed messages!'"

The quest to become an evergreen corporation is ever elusive. Companies that take these five imperatives to heart are more likely to stay on top, avoiding the success trap and positioning themselves to shape their future.

Martin Reeves, Gerry Hansell, and Rodolphe Charme di Carlo
Chapter 6
How Vital Companies Think, Act, and Thrive

Vitality shows in not only the ability to persist but the ability to start over.

–F. Scott Fitzgerald

How do you keep the vitality of day one, even inside a large organization?　　*–Jeff Bezos*

Leadership has its benefits – scale, knowledge, influence, and financial stability among them. But our research shows that as companies age and grow, incumbents increasingly focus on internal matters, have more difficulty freeing themselves from legacy businesses and approaches, and progressively shift their priorities toward running – rather than reinventing – the business. Nontraditional competitors, disruptive technologies, and new business models are making corporate reinvention a critical priority.

How can legacy leaders remain vital – to preserve and develop their capacity for growth, risk taking, innovation, and long-term success? In creating a quantitative measure of corporate vitality and its underlying drivers, we hope to provide a working framework of what matters when managing the balance between delivering near-term execution and investing in the future. The drive to maintain vitality has organizational, financial, and cultural levers – all of which reinforce each other.

Vitality: A Necessity for Long-Term Growth

The challenge is straightforward: Growth is critical for sustained value creation. In the short term, companies can create value by optimizing costs or assets or by building investors' expectations. Yet in the long run, most value creation comes from top-line growth, which accounts for 74% of total shareholder return of S&P 500 top-quartile-performing companies over a ten-year period (Figure 6.1).

The good news is that achieving sustainable growth is still possible for today's incumbents. Approximately 10% of large US companies are growing at double-digit rates (Figure 6.2). Among that 10%, many – such as Visa and Mastercard (credit cards), Hilton (hotels), Constellation Brands (alcoholic beverages), and O'Reilly (auto parts) – are from nontech industries. What is their secret?

https://doi.org/10.1515/9783110745511-006

Sources of TSR among top-quartile S&P 500 companies

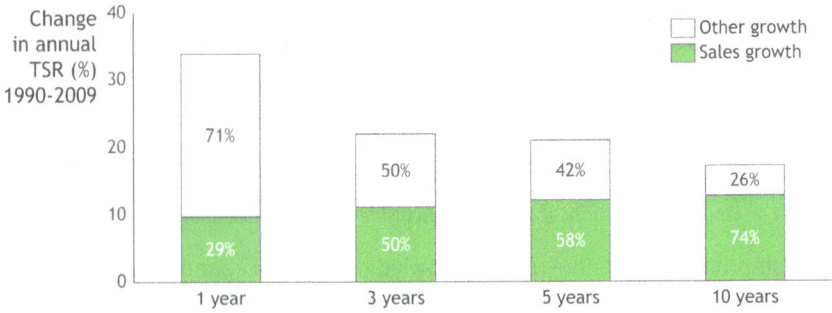

Source: BCG Henderson Institute analysis

Figure 6.1: Most value creation comes from top-line growth.

5-year growth distribution by market capitalization

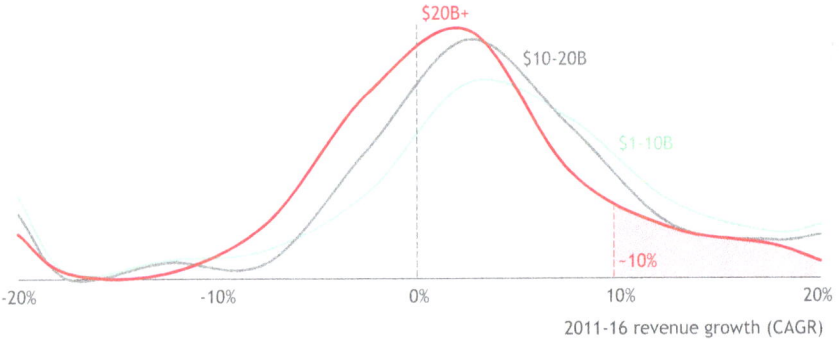

1. Market cap as of 2011 (beginning of sample) | Note: US companies excluding energy.
Source: BCG Henderson Institute

Figure 6.2: Approximately 10% of large US companies are growing at double-digit rates.

In today's rapidly changing environment – with elevated political, social, and technological uncertainty – what will make a company thrive tomorrow is different from what makes it succeed today. Current performance is less and less predictive, and an overreliance on backward-looking metrics can be deceptive. Many of today's large incumbents are vulnerable, even if they have a solid track record of past performance.

And abrupt failures happen increasingly frequently – think Kodak or Blockbuster – in no small part because of the risk of digital disruption.[1] Even when their positions seem comfortable, incumbents need to create a sense of urgency[2] and preemptively address the requirements to sustained success. They must develop their capacity for growth and reinvention. This is what we call *vitality*.

We are able to measure vitality by using BCG's proprietary methodology behind the Fortune Future 50[3] – the result of a two-year research partnership between BCG and *Fortune* magazine. This index ranks the most vital US-listed companies. To build it, we collected all theories purporting to explain the ability of a company to grow and we associated them with measurable variables. We then tested those theories against historical data and only kept the variables that had a measurable and robust impact on long-term revenue growth. As expected, the age and size of a company have a negative impact on growth – confirming that the more established the incumbent, the harder it is to remain vital.

We were also able to identify these key building blocks for vital companies (Figure 6.3):

- **The ability to continuously develop future growth options.** This is the main driver of vitality for incumbents. It can be achieved by constantly renewing a pipeline of potential bets, catalyzed by an entrepreneurial spirit that facilitates ongoing exploration – even when the fruits of a previous exploration are in the midst of paying off.
- **The willingness of leadership to think differently about strategy.** Unlike the companies that are narrowly focused on maximizing short-term total shareholder return,[4] leaders of vital incumbents are focused on exploration[5] and have a long-term orientation. We know this because we trained a natural-language-processing algorithm on 70,000 annual reports filed by companies to the US Securities and Exchange Commission. This enabled us to detect future-oriented strategic thinking and demonstrate that it is positively correlated with long-term revenue growth.

---

1 https://www.nacdonline.org/analytics/survey.cfm?ItemNumber=66753
2 https://www.linkedin.com/pulse/creating-urgency-amidst-comfort-leadership-agenda-2018-reeves/
3 https://fortune.com/future-50/
4 https://www.washingtonpost.com/business/economy/maximizing-shareholder-value-the-goal-that-changed-corporate-america/2013/08/26/26e9ca8e-ed74-11e2-9008-61e94a7ea20d_story.html?utm_term=.cb9adbd7f16e
5 https://www.bcg.com/publications/2017/think-biologically-messy-management-for-complex-world

Source: BCG Henderson Institute

Figure 6.3: Key building blocks of a vital company.

Furthermore, leaders must drive this long-term orientation into the organization, by promoting "day one" mentality,[6] for example, and allocating sufficient resources to place and evolve bets. Thornton Tomasetti, a leading engineering firm, embraces this mindset fully in its five-year strategic vision: "We keep our eyes and minds open, test new ideas thoroughly, and invest selectively and quickly."

– **The determination to build the right capabilities.** Strategy and execution cannot be separated from one another,[7] and to be vital, companies need to build the right capabilities – especially in relation to technology and people. Vital incumbents are able to stay on top of relevant emerging technology, in part by using transformative (as opposed to scale- and cost-driven) M&A moves when needed. They employ "post-merger rejuvenation" to acquire smaller, faster-growing companies and inject new capabilities and stimulate growth (Chapter 12).

In addition, the most vital companies maintain a diverse and youthful organization at all levels – including within the boardroom – by providing leadership opportunities for upcoming talent. Our research[8] shows that there is a

---

6 https://fortune.com/2016/03/25/jeff-bezos-beginners-mind/?utm_source=fortune.com&utm_medium=email&utm_campaign=data-sheet&utm_content=2017121114pm

7 https://hbr.org/2017/11/your-strategy-has-to-be-flexible-but-so-does-your-execution

8 https://hbr.org/2018/01/how-and-where-diversity-drives-financial-performance

statistically significant relationship between innovation and diversity in its many dimensions.

The Challenge of Ambidexterity

Vitality alone is not enough for incumbents to thrive and grow sustainably. Overperformance within the core business is also necessary in order to finance vitality. Even if having deeper pockets is a potential advantage for incumbents, they must still work at realizing ambidexterity – being able to run and reinvent the company at the same time (Figure 6.4).

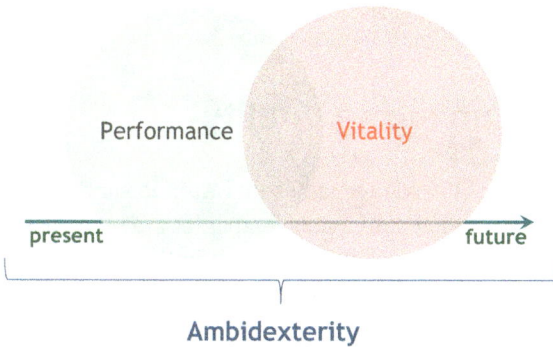

Source: BCG Henderson Institute

Figure 6.4: Companies need to be able to run and reinvent at the same time.

Embracing the contradiction of ambidexterity – optimizing current performance while building the potential for long-term growth – is difficult for any company. This is especially true for incumbents, where the current business model can easily dominate resources, talent, and thinking. The most obvious impediment to ambidexterity for incumbents is sheer size, and there are several factors that can turn the benefits of scale into the burden of inertia.

First, as companies grow older, successful behaviors from the past tend to ossify into fixed thinking and processes, as well as specialized talent. Leaders can be part of the problem, since they are likely to be associated with, and personally invested in, the current model of success.

Second, slower decision making and an aversion to risk can be harmful in their own right and also make it more difficult to attract and retain entrepreneurial talent.

Third, companies focused on exploitation – or current performance – have a tendency toward *financialization*: decisions are based predominantly on financial metrics, such as profitability or earnings per share. Exploration might look unattractive or poorly defined when judged by the crisp financial metrics possible for a mature business. The risk-weighted returns on individual exploratory investments might be low or difficult to quantify, but when considered collectively they can be essential for the continued existence of the company. The best way to assess whether a bet is worth the risk may sometimes be to compare it with a scenario of the eventual demise of the cash-cow business.

Finally, having a strong TSR track record and a generous dividend policy can also increase investors' expectations of continued short-term cash returns. This can narrow management focus toward optimizing short-term financial wins over long-term investments – that is, performance over vitality.

Three Steps Toward Enhancing Vitality

Building vitality is essential for established companies that want to survive and thrive. Even when measuring short-term health, vital companies are in the lead. From 2011 through 2016, the top 10% most vital incumbents in the Fortune Future 50 outperformed their peers by 5% per year in growth and 10% per year in TSR (Figure 6.5).

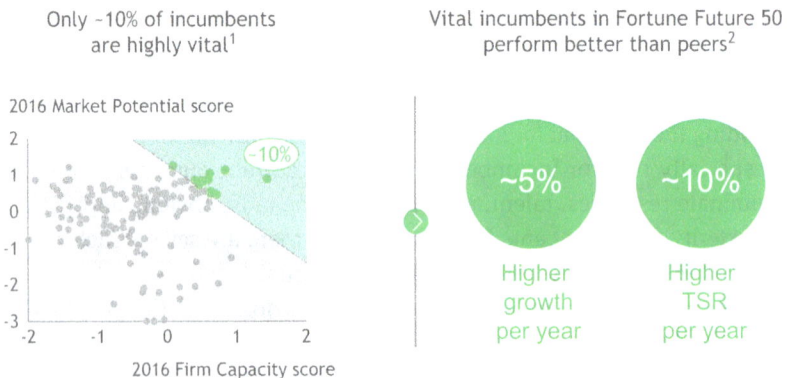

Only ~10% of incumbents are highly vital[1]

2016 Market Potential score

2016 Firm Capacity score

Vital incumbents in Fortune Future 50 perform better than peers[2]

~5% Higher growth per year

~10% Higher TSR per year

1. Incumbents = firms older than avg. (40+ years old) with $20B+ mkt cap 2. vs. all other incumbents; 3. 5-year period of 12/31/2011 through 12/31/2016 Note: Excludes energy companies. Source: BCG Henderson Institute

Figure 6.5: The most vital incumbents outperformed their peers by 5% per year in growth and 10% per year in TSR.

To become a more vital organization, company leaders must follow three steps.

Step 1: Assess Your Current Vitality

Establish a clear understanding of your starting point from the outside in and from the inside out, by answering the following questions:
- What is the growth potential of your pipeline of "future bets"?
- To what extent does your strategy encompass long-term exploration?
- What are you doing to develop leading capabilities in technology?
- Are you willing to challenge the approaches and beliefs that have historically made you successful?
- Are you taking a risk on new talent, and is your organization cognitively diverse?

Step 2: Strengthen or Renew Sources of Vitality

This can include a range of measures:
- **Create a portfolio of growth options.** Companies need to have a balanced portfolio of bets on different timescales. In order to do this, they must develop a tolerance for failure and create incentives for entrepreneurship.

  Recruit, one of Japan's most successful large companies in recent times (20% growth per year in the last five years), embodies this culture perfectly. Through its New Ring program, which receives more than 1,000 proposals every year, Recruit allows any employee, sometimes in collaboration with outside stakeholders, to propose starting a new business in line with the company's hybrid ecosystem philosophy.[9] By doing so, leadership is able to systematically identify, nurture, and celebrate entrepreneurial talent within the company.
- **Build adaptive and shaping capabilities.** Incumbents often have strongly developed capabilities to deal with classical strategy and execution,[10] which is powerful and necessary in mature businesses. But the uncertain environment of many emerging businesses requires a more adaptive approach to

---

9 https://www.bcg.com/publications/2017/business-model-innovation-technology-digital-getting-physical-rise-hybrid-ecosystems
10 https://hbr.org/2012/09/your-strategy-needs-a-strategy

strategy and execution. This requires, for instance, a system to seed, test, and scale new ideas in a rapid and iterative fashion.

In addition, shaping capabilities enable incumbents to influence their business environment rather than be at its mercy. These include the ability to conceive and create new markets, mobilize others around new win-win propositions, create and orchestrate collaborative ecosystems, and allow these ecosystems to evolve as circumstances change. A famous example is Apple's transformation of the smartphone market. It triumphed against incumbent players by building an ecosystem of collaborators that together could create a smartphone and a rich library of software, instead of attempting to build everything internally.

– **Invest in technology.** Technology capabilities are even more important than one might imagine. Our analysis shows that a common feature of the least vital incumbents is the weakness of their technology portfolio. At the other end of the spectrum, Mastercard illustrates how having a strong emphasis on technology can help incumbents evolve and thrive. Mastercard has shifted from being a payments company to also becoming a technology leader, as expressed through its mission: "We're providing the technology that's leading the way toward a world beyond cash."[11]

– **Maintain dynamism and diversity.** Compositional diversity is not enough. Diversity of employee backgrounds favors but does not guarantee innovation. Also necessary is an environment that is conducive to encouraging diversity of thought and a collision of ideas. Thornton Tomasetti's five-year strategic vision states, "Everyone contributes to learning, and new ideas are given a chance."

There are several other ways to broaden an organization's thinking, including maverick scans[12] and scenario-based stress tests. In addition, using a flat, adaptive structure as well as team-based leadership helps to foster further diversity of thought. The more fluid an organization, the more it allows people to self-organize around new ideas and better ways of doing things. For example, Morningstar Foods has adopted an extreme "no-hierarchy" structure[13] that allows for "a lot of spontaneous innovation and ideas for change [to] come from unusual places."

---

11 https://www.mastercard.us/en-us.html

12 https://www.bcg.com/publications/2013/strategy-growth-lessons-from-mavericks-staying-big-acting-small

13 https://hbr.org/2011/12/first-lets-fire-all-the-managers

- **Self-disrupt *before* being disrupted.** Recent research shows that only one-third of incumbents facing disruption survive and thrive.[14] Survival depends on preemptively creating a sense of urgency and a will to self-disrupt before being disrupted.
- **Self-disruption can either happen internally or through M&A moves.** The former requires boldly rethinking the business model, while building on existing advantages. Restructuring to separate or divest legacy businesses can be part of the solution, too. Otherwise, incumbents can look outside and consider acquiring – or *acqui-hiring* – disruptive and emerging companies. This can result in postmerger rejuvenation,[15] as happened to Disney when it used Pixar as a stimulus for self-disruption, learning, and ultimately growth.

Step 3: Lead with Ambidexterity

Leaders need to ensure their businesses are capable of performing well in the present as well as developing future potential, by leveraging the following checklist:
- **Choose the right approach to strategy for each part of the business.** Mature core businesses require very different approaches to strategy and execution than emerging ones do. As laid out in *Your Strategy Needs a Strategy*,[16] the approach to strategy and execution needs to be flexible, based on the business environment that each part of the business faces.
- **Structure to enable multiple approaches.** Ambidexterity enables firms to deploy different approaches to strategy simultaneously in each part of the business and manage the resulting contradictions. As a result, ambidextrous firms are able to perform strongly and be vital at the same time. This is particularly challenging for incumbents, but adopting the right organizational structure can help.

    The Chinese consumer-goods company Haier, which went from near-bankruptcy in the 1980s to its global market leader position today, is a powerful example of how adjusting organizational structure can be the path to ambidexterity. How did Haier do it? In an effort to improve its ability to deliver customer value, the conglomerate flattened its organization and developed

---

14 https://www.bcg.com/publications/2017/value-creation-strategy-transformation-creating-value-disruption-others-disappear
15 https://www.bcg.com/publications/2016/postmerger-rejuvenation
16 https://store.hbr.org/product/your-strategy-needs-a-strategy-how-to-choose-and-execute-the-right-approach/14054?sku=14054-HBK-ENG

2,000 self-governing units. This drastic change enabled each unit to function like an autonomous company and use an approach to strategy tailored to its specific situation.

– **Manage the "investor story."** As a response to short-term-oriented investor pressures, incumbent leadership needs to convince investors that current performance is on track and the business case for future investment is sound. This is a very important step in buying time and permission to strengthen vitality.

Andrew Wilson, CEO of Electronic Arts, gave a presentation to investors[17] that exemplifies how a forward-looking vision should be communicated. He started by emphasizing the positive short-term and midterm financial outlook driven by the core portfolio and then laid out an inspirational long-term-growth strategy focused on new portfolio bets, new geographic expansion, and business model innovation.

Incumbent businesses are at a crossroads. Short-term performance is strong overall, but political, social, and technological change and uncertainty cloud the horizon. Thus, the prize for being vital is more valuable than ever. With equal emphasis on performance and vitality, companies can thrive into the future.

---

17 https://ir.ea.com/home/default.aspx

Knut Haanæs, Martin Reeves, and Jules Wurlod
Chapter 7
The 2% Company

Very few companies can excel at innovation and efficiency at the same time. Of the 2,500 public companies we analyzed, just 2% consistently outperform their peers on both growth and profitability during good *and* bad times. These "2% companies," as we call them, are able to renew themselves in large part by driving innovation and efficiency simultaneously. All ambitious companies should, in our opinion, strive to become 2% companies – which are positioned to succeed over time and thrive during both turbulent and nonturbulent periods.

Being excellent at both exploration (new ideas and innovation) and exploitation (operational proficiency and efficiency) simultaneously is difficult because these activities are contradictory – they pull companies in different directions. They require different skills, different performance management, and an ability to drive success with different time perspectives. They are also potential traps, each in its own way. For example, pursuing too much innovation tempts companies to seek further change before they see the benefits of the initial change. Conversely, operational success today makes it more difficult to change and explore.

The 2% companies take varied approaches to exploration and exploitation and thus manifest themselves in different ways (Figure 7.1). Three examples:
- The fashion retailer Zara has developed "fast fashion" DNA that combines adaptive innovation and speed-to-store. Zara consistently taps into unpredictable changes in taste through excellence in design agility and fosters continuous improvements in efficiency through a very tight supply chain.
- Amazon is also a 2% company, but it manifests this status differently. Amazon has been visionary since its founding, rolling out a global marketplace for its expanding customer base. From the top, CEO Jeff Bezos constantly pushes for a culture of innovative thinking through his "day one" mantra, stressing how the company should never stop being a startup. In parallel, the global retailer is able to drive efficiency by building an ever-tighter customer insight, logistics, and delivery operation.
- Toyota is another 2% company, here manifested through a long-term quest to develop new products (such as hybrid engines) and new ways of using materials and by continuously improving its lean manufacturing system. By playing the long game, Toyota has shown that gradual improvements in quality and manufacturing can be combined with breakthrough innovation and industry shaping.

https://doi.org/10.1515/9783110745511-007

All three companies excel at both innovation and efficiency: the hallmark of the 2% company.

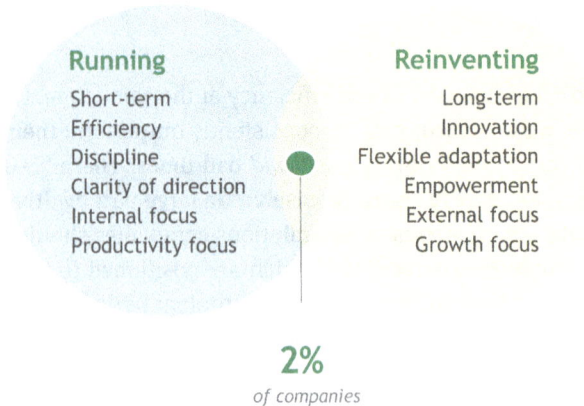

Running

Short-term
Efficiency
Discipline
Clarity of direction
Internal focus
Productivity focus

Reinventing

Long-term
Innovation
Flexible adaptation
Empowerment
External focus
Growth focus

2%
of companies

Source: BCG Henderson Institute

Figure 7.1: The 2% companies are capable of both exploration and exploitation.

Traits of 2% Companies

The 2% companies share four traits:

1. These companies are **excellent at both exploration and exploitation**. They continually rethink and revise their strategies and operating models while improving their current products and operations.
2. They **retain an "outside in" focus even when successful**. By bringing outside perspectives in, they avoid succumbing to the risks posed by success and growth, which, although they are positive and desired outcomes, tend to increase organizational complexity and push companies toward an internal focus. In a rapidly changing environment, any company with too much of an inward gaze will fail to detect fundamental external market changes.
3. The 2% companies **embrace necessary disruptions** (even painful ones). This also implies deprioritizing profitable businesses to bet on future growth areas and build early-mover advantages.
4. They have a **clear model for renewal**. Renewal models help to manage the inevitable trade-offs between short- and long-term objectives. They also fit specific business environments and organizational capabilities. For instance, in industries where disruption is imminent but directionally unclear and

when go-to-market capabilities are strong, companies can capitalize on innovation from outside by scanning the market for relevant innovations, bringing them in-house, and commercializing them. This allows them to build an early-mover advantage while avoiding the risk of going full-steam in the wrong direction.

Excellence in Exploration and Exploitation

On the one hand, exploitation activities focus on short-term improvements and refinement of existing knowledge. Capitalizing on current opportunities has the advantage of providing payoffs that are imminent and that offer greater certainty. On the other hand, exploration activities (new ideas and innovation) are linked to the longer term and represent the search for new opportunities. Exploration is necessary to build the knowledge to cope with disruption risks and to seize new opportunities, which is fundamental for long-term success.

Most companies aren't good at both, because these two areas require very different skills. The short-term focus on cost, efficiency, and process improvement is fundamentally at odds with the long-term need for innovation, experimentation, and risk taking. Despite this inherent tension, both viewpoints are critical for sustainable business success.

The 2% companies manage to be excellent at both, which in practice means that they avoid two traps: the perpetual-search trap and the success trap.

Companies mired in the *perpetual-search trap* do not have the patience to wait for the payback on exploration because realizing value from exploration is both time-consuming and uncertain. The diffusion of new ideas is often an S-shaped curve, which means that innovations can take time to reach critical mass and yield any substantial profits. If companies make projections based on the very short term, prospects will always look unfavorable. In fact, applying a short-term perspective to exploration makes almost all new ideas look bad.

The *success trap*, conversely, is associated with too much exploitation. That is the case when a company is satisfied by the returns on exploiting present knowledge and technologies. Its current success will tempt the company to continue exploiting, at the expense of exploration – although exploration is necessary in the long term. We found that fully one-third of companies fall into the success trap during a five-year period and that only one in five manages to escape.

In the long run, the best performers are companies that are able to do both: to foster efficiency and to explore future growth options.

Maintaining an "Outside in" Focus Even When Successful

Disruption usually comes from the outside, and being too inward-looking puts companies at risk of missing key customer or market trends. The 2% companies don't just excel at both exploration and exploitation activities, they also manage to keep an external (outside-in) focus even when they are successful. This is not as easy as it seems – successful companies very often become introverted. History is paved with examples of companies that reached the top of their industry but failed to remain there, for example, Motorola, Blockbuster, Dell, Nokia, and Kodak.

Some current industry leaders, flush with current success, might be overlooking emerging threats. Traditional banks, for example, may be underestimating fintechs. The fintech industry has exploded over the last decade and is now worth an estimated £7 billion in the UK alone. A recent report by the Bank of England found that traditional banks believe they can cope with fintech competition without making big changes to their business models or taking on more risk – but also that fintechs may cause "greater and faster disruption" to banks' business models than the banks themselves project.[1]

One reason for an inward shift could be complexity. Successful companies have a tendency to gradually become inward facing because organizational complexity has increased. When successful companies grow, so do the breadth and depth of business requirements. As a response, companies tend to create dedicated structures, processes, systems, and metrics that make the organization more complicated. Significant resources and attention must then be devoted to internal management.

Success can also make companies look inward because, by generating too much free cash flow for allocation, success can exacerbate an agency problem: managers might push to keep as many resources as possible under their control and thus invest all extra cash in projects in-house, while, in contrast, board members might want to maximize the payoff for shareholders and thus avoid investing in projects that gradually become less attractive according to the law of diminishing returns.

Maintaining an outside-in drive starts by continuously scanning the market, both demand and supply. On the demand side, successful companies must see themselves through the eyes of the customer and constantly look out for

---

1 Bank of England, *Stress Testing the UK Banking System: 2017 Results*, November 2017. The report is based on a stress test of seven major banks in the UK: HSBC, Barclays, Lloyds Bank, the Royal Bank of Scotland, Santander UK, Standard Chartered, and Nationwide.

early signs of potential megatrends. On the supply side, companies must be willing and able to engage in partnerships and collaborations.

For example, in 2011, Umicore, a Belgian metals and mining company, wanted to expand its recycling activities in order to recover rare earth elements from rechargeable batteries. The company possessed a state-of-the-art battery-recycling process – the Ultra High Temperature (UHT) process – but lacked the capabilities to refine rare earths. It thus partnered with Rhodia, a French chemical company. Together, the two companies developed the first industrial process that closed the loop on the rare earths contained in batteries.

Breakthrough innovation is rarely performed by one single actor end-to-end, and participation in relevant partnerships, platforms, or ecosystems can be key.

Embracing Disruption

When disruptive shocks hit, they must be fully embraced. Doing so first requires companies to recognize the risks. Strategic decision making in the context of risk can be subject to multiple cognitive biases. One example is loss aversion, in which the thought of losing something one already has is more abhorrent than not taking advantage of a new opportunity for gain. Therefore, there is a tendency to overvalue current business models compared with new, disruptive models and their opportunities. To sidestep that problem, companies must be brutally honest and recognize that market conditions won't remain the same forever – they never do. Profitable businesses inevitably attract potential entrants with innovative business models.

In practice, fully embracing disruption means that at times companies must respond by being disruptive themselves rather than making small incremental fixes to their current model.

Tobacco companies understood this when they invested – massively – in electronic cigarettes. Electronic cigarettes have been around for nearly 30 years but gained strong momentum only recently, pushed by small emerging players such as V2, Juul, and Mig Vapor. Large tobacco companies decided to embrace disruption by bringing to market their own solutions. Philip Morris International (PMI), for example, invested about $3 billion to develop its iQOS. The company has done so despite the high cannibalization risk to its current business.[2] In fact,

---

2 The disruptive risk posed by electronic cigarettes is material: they are most popular among young smokers, and specialists believe that young people who miss the early tobacco habit may never become traditional smokers, given that nine out of ten adult tobacco smokers began smoking by age 18 and that nearly all began smoking by age 25.

PMI's CEO, André Calantzopoulos, even declared, in late 2017, that this new technology will eventually fully replace traditional cigarettes. (Admittedly, this statement might have been motivated in part by public-image concerns.)

Another example involves the introduction of mobile technologies. When telecom companies faced the entrance of mobile technologies, they could have responded either by incrementally refining their old landline business or by using those innovative mobile technologies themselves to become part of the disruptive force. In the longer term, only the latter approach allowed companies to realize the full benefits of disruption.

Overall, when disruption hits, major commitments have to be made, even if doing so is painful. These commitments can also mean deprioritizing profitable activities to focus resources – management attention, talent, or financial resources – on disruptive trends. Neste, a Finnish oil-refining company, invested heavily in renewable-diesel production, foreseeing regulatory changes in the EU that would create a market for diesel made from renewable sources. The firm developed technology that allows it to produce diesel from vegetable oils and waste animal fats. With this technology, it is possible to slash CO_2 emissions by 40% to 60% compared with its fossil-fuel-based counterpart. This strategy paid off. In 2015, Neste was the largest producer of renewable fuels from waste and residues worldwide. In 2016, thanks to high margins, renewable products reached close to 50% of the company's total operating margin, for approximately 20% of total revenue.

Having the Right Model for Renewal

The 2% companies have an explicit model for managing the inevitable trade-offs between near- and long-term priorities. The right model for the subsequent renewal also optimally leverages the capabilities of the company and fits the organizational culture. Needless to say, these models are company-specific and there is no "one size fits all." In our work with various industries and in ongoing discussions with executives, we've identified a set of models. A few examples:

- **The Freeze Timeframe Model.** In this model, companies define a specific time horizon and operate within this window to optimize their existing product portfolio and pursue exploration activities accordingly. This can be a good strategy if, for example, management has limited long-term priorities, can predict the near future fairly confidently, has the resources to invest in the desired product enhancements, and believes that building these enhancements up front will deliver a competitive advantage. Private equity firms are good examples of businesses that invest to create value in a defined time window, usually approximately three to five years. When taking on a company, they will do the exploration that creates visible value in the medium term.

- **The No-Regrets Model.** This strategy means making sure that your company encounters no surprises in its market domain. Companies need to identify the domain they are playing in and then, within it, engage a wide variety of technological options. By adopting this strategy, companies guarantee an early-mover advantage whatever winning option the market ultimately picks. Companies need to be able to recognize winners early by picking up weak signals. A case in point: Essilor, the world leader in eyeglass lenses, has proved that it can stay successful by continuously scanning and engaging with all novelties in its domain that can change the industry. With this strategy, the company has successfully caught multiple innovation waves, such as online retailing, plastic lenses, sunglasses, and low-cost manufacturing in Asia.
- **The Commercializer Model.** Companies do not always have a monopoly on good ideas. The commercializer model implies scanning outside for relevant products developed externally, bringing them in-house, and then commercializing them. This strategy requires strong go-to-market capabilities and the resources necessary to acquire the targets identified. It also rests on the ability to scan the market for relevant opportunities and recognize them early, before their market value shoots up. To some extent, this strategy complements a strong in-house innovation engine. Most big pharma companies rely on this model to supplement their own drug pipelines, for instance. By in-licensing products that are already fairly well developed, getting FDA approval, and taking them to market quickly, pharma companies can ensure a steady stream of new products with faster time to market and lower R&D risks.
- **The Win-Stay/Lose-Shift Model.** Another model is to gather, screen, and test many ideas quickly, with minimal financial investment in each. This diversified strategy can be far less risky than one big bet-the-farm commitment. But it requires the company to identify early the ideas that are less promising and to "fail fast" before too many resources are spent. It therefore necessitates clear criteria and metrics and disciplined objectivity. Once a winner is identified, the company also needs the capabilities to quickly scale up. Zara, the fashion company, typically masters this model. Another good example is Amgen: the biotech company used to fund as many drugs as possible and hope for the best. Now, although Amgen's R&D strategy still focuses only on breakthrough drugs, the company evaluates drugs quickly, weeding out candidates that don't make the grade. This fail-fast approach saved the company $1 billion in research spending on just a single drug.
- **The Innovation Platform Model.** Some companies are able to create an attractive technology platform on which other companies can build their

businesses. Amazon and Alibaba have made this strategy work, providing partners with tools, data, and other services to help online businesses succeed. Key success factors here include a truly differentiated platform, cutting-edge technology, the satisfaction of merchants and business partners, and the continuous incorporation of new ideas and improvements – there has to be a clear reason why an outside business would use your platform rather than taking products to market themselves or through others.

Recommendations for Top Management

We offer five recommendations for becoming a 2% company:

1. **Invite challenge and coaching from the outside.** Welcome differing opinions. Be willing to be challenged by, and to learn from, others. No one can be right all the time, and welcoming outsiders so that you can benefit from their unbiased, outside-in perspectives will help you stay close to customers and nascent market trends. Having a clear picture of those trends will also prevent your company from setting out in a wrong direction and provides the confidence necessary to make difficult decisions.

2. **Think in multiple time frames.** Ask yourself what you're doing to best position yourself for next year, five years from now, and ten years from now. This mindset will enable both exploration and exploitation activities and strike the right balance of the two. Thinking in multiple time frames is also a critical first step toward defining the right renewal model for your company, as it ensures that your chosen strategy will deliver results at all relevant time frames.

3. **Get ahead of any crisis.** Recognize risk and be brutally honest. Once risks and opportunities have been clearly identified, make sure you address disruption in the way that best positions your company and takes full advantage of the disruptive forces. Have the courage to act promptly and preemptively: establish an early-mover advantage that can be instrumental for sustainable success.

4. **Be skeptical of current** success. One should never rest on one's laurels. Successful companies must stay sober and modest to avoid creating a company culture that rests on complacency and self-satisfaction. Rather, keep a mindset of continuous quest for improvement and search for novel ideas. This will trickle down through the entire organization and ensure that key stakeholders always push the frontier of possibilities.

Are we addressing disruption?

1. Embracing disruption

Action

Reality

0.0   5.0

Reality > Action

2. Balancing exploration and exploitation

Action

Intent

0.0   5.0

Intent > Action

How are we addressing disruption?

3. Remaining outside-in

Action

Intent

0.0   5.0

Intent > Action

4. Fitting renewal model to business footprint

Model/ footprint fit

0.0   5.0

Model = Footprint

5. Organizational alignment

Alignment score

Summary

- ❶ Embracing disruption
- ❷ Balancing exploration and exploitation
- ❸ Remaining outside-in
- ❹ Fitting renewal model to business footprint
- ❺ Organizational alignment

······ Intent   ——— Action

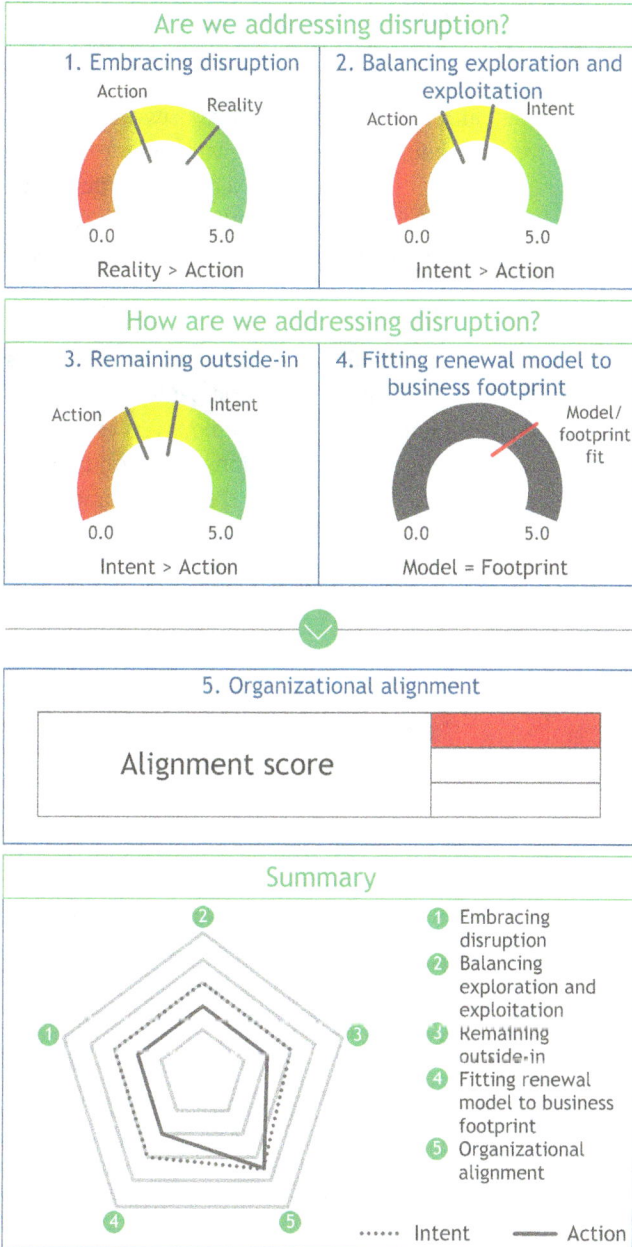

Source BCG analysis

Figure 7.2: The 2% cockpit assessment tool.

5. **Review your renewal strategies explicitly.** Pursuing excellence on all four of the previously described traits can be exhausting for an organization. As a result, explicitly reviewing your company's performance is necessary to ensure that all dimensions are tackled and that there are no gaps between intention and action. To this end, we have built a simple, pragmatic assessment tool that helps executives to rapidly weigh their strategies against the four traits. We call it the "2% cockpit" because it helps to show executives how to pilot their organizations the way that 2% companies do. Figure 7.2 is a sample cockpit view.

The 2% companies set a high bar. But by emulating these performance leaders and heeding the recommendations set forth above, other companies can achieve and sustain a higher level of success than they currently enjoy. Ten years from now, we may find ourselves talking about new manifestations of exploration and exploitation and an expanded roster of companies that excel at both innovation and efficiency: the 3% – or more.

Martin Reeves, Knut Haanæs, James Hollingsworth,
and Filippo Scognamiglio

Chapter 8
Ambidexterity: The Art of Thriving
in Complex Environments

To deliver growth among the best in our industry, we're strengthening our core business, re-newing our focus on discontinuous innovation, and implementing a $10 billion productivity program. — Procter & Gamble, 2012 Annual Report

Managers today face an apparent contradiction. On one hand, austerity in the developed world and intense competition push them to cut costs and drive efficiencies. On the other, the increasing pace of change means they need to emphasize innovation.

Resolving this contradiction requires *ambidexterity* – the ability to both explore new avenues and exploit existing ones. Companies need ambidexterity when operating in diverse environments that require different styles of strategy simultaneously, or in dynamic environments that require them to transition between styles over time.[1] Companies need to be ambidextrous when operating in both emerging and developed markets, when bringing new products and technologies to market while exploiting existing ones, when integrating startups into their existing business, and in a range of other circumstances.

The need to develop ambidexterity is widely acknowledged: in a BCG survey of 130 senior executives of major public and private companies, fully 90 percent agreed that being able to manage multiple strategy styles and transition between them was an important capability to develop. But this aspiration is hard to realize. Exploration and exploitation require different ways of organizing and managing. Exploration is facilitated by long-term targets, a flexible and decentralized structure, and a culture of autonomy and risk taking, while exploitation typically requires short-term targets, centralization, standardization, and discipline in execution. Switching between them is difficult because managers tend to emphasize what delivered success yesterday. In the words of BCG's founder, Bruce Henderson, "Success in the past always becomes enshrined in the present by the overvaluation of the policies and attitudes which accompanied that success."

---

1 "Your Strategy Needs a Strategy," *Harvard Business Review*, September 2012, https://www.bcg.com/publications/2012/your-strategy-needs-a-strategy.

https://doi.org/10.1515/9783110745511-008

3M, a company renowned for its culture of innovation, experienced the exploration-exploitation trade-off in the early 2000s, when it introduced Six Sigma practices in an effort to boost productivity. While the company's productivity did indeed increase, the same practices reduced 3M's ability to innovate, as evidenced by a fall in the proportion of revenues from new products.

Ambidexterity is therefore rare: a recent BCG study of the financial performance of approximately 2,000 publicly listed U.S. companies found that only about 2 percent consistently outperformed their industry in both turbulent and stable periods. But ambidexterity is becoming an increasingly critical asset as the diversity and dynamism of business environments rise. The growing economic importance of emerging markets, for example, is expanding the range of environments that companies need to operate in. At the same time, technological change is overturning existing products and business models at an increasing rate. It took the PC approximately 15 years to go from 10 percent market penetration to 40 percent; it took the internet 5 years and smartphones fewer than 3.

Picking the Right Approach to Ambidexterity

Companies in stable, simple environments do not require ambidexterity – they can thrive by emphasizing operating efficiency. But most others will need to pursue it. Ambidexterity can be achieved through four distinct approaches: separation, switching, self-organizing, and external ecosystem (Figure 8.1).

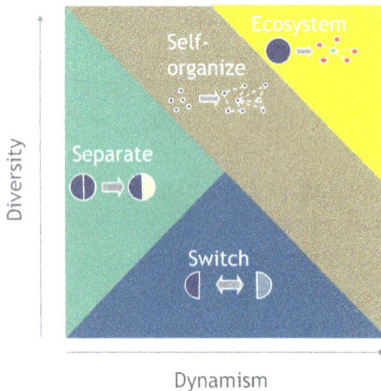

Source: BCG analysis

Figure 8.1: The 4 approaches to achieving ambidexterity.

Separation

Separation is the simplest, most common approach to achieving ambidexterity and is appropriate for companies facing environments that are diverse but relatively stable over time. It involves structurally separating units that need to deploy different strategy styles. A company might, for example, separate its mature business, which requires efficiency and disciplined execution, from its emerging business, which needs to be innovative and flexible.

There are many well-known examples of this approach. In 1943, Lockheed Martin, faced with the task of creating an advanced fighter while at the same time mass producing its established Hudson bomber, opted to create two fully separate units (marking the birth of what would become the company's famous Skunk Works), each with its own physical location, resources, and culture. Similarly, in 2000, IBM separated its established businesses, where a focus on execution and operating metrics was appropriate, from its emerging-businesses unit, which the company used to explore new opportunities and markets.

But separation does not always work, because a company's structure tends to be semipermanent while its environment may not be. Separation also creates barriers that prevent information and resource flow among units, potentially impeding their ability to change emphasis or style when required. Companies such as fashion retailer Zara and industrial conglomerate GE have reduced separation when operating in dynamic environments. At Zara, design and manufacturing work collaboratively to shorten new-product cycles in a highly dynamic industry. GE has in-sourced manufacturing of some of its high-end refrigerators and other consumer appliances and increased integration of design and manufacturing, allowing the business to shift quickly from creating new designs to exploiting them in the market.

Switching

Dynamic environments require instead a *switching* approach. Here, a company changes its style over time as its environment changes, similar to the way in which new companies evolve. Initially, an organization must deploy an exploratory style as it looks for a breakout product, service, or technology. Over time, however, it must transition to a more exploitative style in order to scale up and secure a profitable market position. Amazon was able to rapidly switch from exploration to exploitation. In only two years, it went from exploring (out of Jeff Bezos's garage) the use of the internet for retailing to exploiting and industrializing its operations, opening its first distribution center, and going public.

Many larger companies also deploy switching strategies. The glassmaker Corning was able to rapidly transition from exploring ways to make superstrong glass films to delivering its Gorilla Glass product, now found in more than a billion mobile devices worldwide.

Switching requires resources and information to flow readily across organizational boundaries. This can be problematic because when senior management makes the decision to change styles, some organizations respond slowly, resource conflicts erupt between units, and staff resist the change, fearful of the consequences of moving to a new project that might not succeed. Startups are particularly good at switching – but that does not mean that a similar culture cannot exist in a large organization.

Self-Organizing

When a company needs to deploy multiple styles simultaneously – and the styles are changing over time – a *self-organizing* approach is called for, since managing the switching process in a top-down manner becomes complex and infeasible. Here, individuals or small teams can choose for themselves which style to employ and switch between them over time. Companies achieve self-organizational capabilities by breaking the organization down into small units and creating individualized performance contracts. Each unit negotiates with its peers according to local rules of interaction established by the center and deploys whatever style it thinks will maximize its performance.

Chinese consumer-goods company Haier successfully employs a self-organizing approach (Chapter 6). Seeking to improve its ability to deliver customer value, the global conglomerate flattened its organizational structure and developed 2,000 self-governing units. Each unit functions like an autonomous company, with its own profit-and-loss statement, operations, innovation program, and motivation. This approach has helped Haier go from near bankruptcy in the 1980s to market leadership today.

A self-organizing approach has its drawbacks, however. It incurs significant costs from duplication, the lack of scale of the individual units, and the additional costs of enforcing the local rules of interaction and keeping score. This approach is only appropriate in highly diverse and dynamic environments.

External Ecosystem

In the most complex cases, companies may need to orchestrate a diverse ecosystem of external parties in order to source the strategy styles they require. This is the *external ecosystem* approach. Apple has used it with great success in the smartphone arena, where winning requires multiple strategy styles. For example, content creation and app development require rapid adaptation to changing consumer needs and fast-moving competition, while component manufacturing and assembly are scale intensive and require a more classical approach. The industry is also highly dynamic. Rather than trying to deploy all strategy styles itself, Apple chooses to shape and orchestrate an ecosystem of companies that exercise the strategy styles it needs. It achieves this by creating common platforms, such as the iTunes Store, that are beneficial to all ecosystem participants.

Companies need to employ an external ecosystem approach when the environment is extremely diverse and dynamic and it is hard to produce the required range of styles internally. This approach is only appropriate in the most complex cases because of the high costs and risks of cooperation – the cost of building platforms such as iTunes, the profits the company must give away to incentivize third parties to participate, and the risks associated with dilution of control over the company's operations.

The Path to Ambidexterity

To build ambidexterity, companies must understand the diversity and dynamism of their environment, and choose and implement the appropriate approach. Each approach requires a different set of organizational interventions and implies a different role for the center.

Where *separation* is required, identify scale-driven (that is, exploiting) and innovation-driven (that is, exploring) business units and set clear boundaries between them by separating objectives, resources, talent, and risk management approaches. The role of the center here is to set and maintain these boundaries and provide centralized services as efficiently as possible.

Where *switching* is needed, design incentives to break down silos and encourage collaboration, and create a culture of flexibility among managers. The role of the center is to create alignment between strategy style and environment, and to modulate style over time. Central functions like HR and IT should be flexible enough to meet the changing needs of individual groups over time.

Where *self-organizing* is called for, break down business units and functions into small groups and set local rules of interaction for how units negotiate with each other and how performance will be assessed. Here the role of the center is smaller: its function is to design and implement the local incentives from which the organization will self-assemble.

Where an *external ecosystem* is required, create platforms that are attractive to potential partners, develop a vision around which to orchestrate parties, and rearrange the corporate center as coordinator of the external ecosystem.

Although ambidexterity is tough to master, it is an increasingly critical capability for managers struggling with the apparent paradox of exploring and exploiting. The imperative to achieve ambidexterity will only rise as technological change and economic turbulence increase the diversity and dynamism of the business environment. Far-sighted companies are beginning to build organizations that can both explore and exploit. Managers must act decisively or risk being overtaken by ambidextrous rivals.

Part III: **Reinventing Businesses**

Zhenya Lindgardt, Martin Reeves, George Stalk,
and Michael S. Deimler
Chapter 9
Business Model Innovation

By the late 1990s, Apple's initial pathway to growth was running out of steam. The company's proprietary approach to designing both hardware and software limited it to being a niche player and hampered its ability to compete on price. In 2001, Apple began introducing a series of successful new products and services – the iPod, the iTunes online music service, and the iPhone – that propelled the company to the top of its industry. But the shift wasn't only a matter of product innovation. Apple's success resulted from its ability to define a workable business model for downloading music – something that had eluded the music industry for years.

This combination of product innovation and business model innovation (BMI) put Apple at the center of a market approximately 30 times larger than its original market. It also helped expand the company's share of the traditional computer market, as new customers became so attached to their iPods that they took another look at Apple's computers.[1]

The greater frequency of disruption and dislocation in many industries is shortening business model lifecycles. New global competitors are emerging. Assets and activities are migrating to low-cost countries. Systemic risk is growing as global business becomes increasingly interconnected. Social and ecological constraints on corporate action are emerging. All these factors require businesses to bolster and accelerate innovation. The discipline of BMI offers a fresh way to think about renewing competitive advantage and reigniting growth in this challenging environment.

Business model innovation means more than a brilliant insight coming at the right place and the right time. To confer a reliable competitive advantage, BMI must be systematically cultivated, sufficiently supported, and explicitly managed. In this chapter, we will discuss the relevance of BMI in the current business environment, describe some of the circumstances in which BMI has proved valuable, identify common pitfalls, and discuss how companies can develop a competitive capability in BMI.

---

1 See *Convergence 2.0: Will You Thrive, Survive, or Fade Away?*, BCG Focus, April 2007; and *Searching for Sustainability: Value Creation in an Era of Diminished Expectations*, BCG report, October 2009.

https://doi.org/10.1515/9783110745511-009

What is Business Model Innovation?

A business model consists of two essential elements – the *value proposition* and the *operating model* – each of which has three sub elements (Figure 9.1).

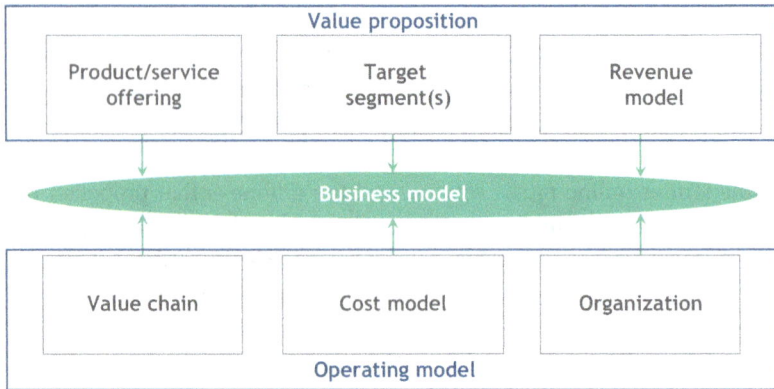

Source: BCG research

Figure 9.1: The elements of a business model.

The **value proposition** answers the question, what are we offering to whom? It reflects explicit choices along the following three dimensions:

1. *Target Segment(s).* Which customers do we choose to serve? Which of their needs do we seek to address?
2. *Product or Service Offering.* What are we offering the customers to satisfy their needs?
3. *Revenue Model.* How are we compensated for our offering?
4. The **operating model** answers the question, how do we profitably deliver the offering? It captures the business's choices in the following three critical areas:
5. *Value Chain.* How are we configured to deliver on customer demand? What do we do in-house? What do we outsource?
6. *Cost Model.* How do we configure our assets and costs to deliver on our value proposition profitably?
7. *Organization.* How do we deploy and develop our people to sustain and enhance our competitive advantage?

As Apple has demonstrated, innovation in a business model is more than mere product, service, or technological innovation. It goes beyond single-function strategies, such as enhancing the sourcing approach or the sales model. Innovation becomes BMI when two or more elements of a business model are reinvented to deliver value in a new way. Because it involves a multidimensional and orchestrated set of activities, BMI is both challenging to execute and difficult to imitate.

Distinguishing business model innovation from product, service, or technology innovations is important. Companies that confuse the latter for the former risk underestimating the requirements for success.

Why Business Model Innovation is Relevant Today

Business model innovation is especially valuable in times of instability. BMI can provide companies a way to break out of intense competition, under which product or process innovations are easily imitated, competitors' strategies have converged, and sustained advantage is elusive. It can help address disruptions – such as regulatory or technological shifts – that demand fundamentally new competitive approaches.

BMI can also help address downturn-specific opportunities, enabling companies, for example, to lower prices or reduce the risks and costs of ownership for customers. In our experience, the companies that flourish in downturns frequently do so by leveraging the crisis to reinvent themselves – rather than by simply deploying defensive financial and operational tactics (Chapter 3). Moreover, during times of crisis, companies often find it easier to gain consensus around the bold moves required to reconfigure an existing business.

BMI may be more challenging than product or process innovation, but it also delivers superior returns. BCG and *BusinessWeek* conducted an annual survey to identify the most innovative companies and segmented the database of innovators into business model innovators, and product or process innovators. Our analysis showed that while both types of innovators achieved a premium over the average total shareholder return for their industries, business model innovators earned an average premium that was more than four times greater than that enjoyed by product or process innovators. Furthermore, BMI delivered returns that were more sustainable; even after ten years, business model innovators continued to outperform competitors and product and process innovators (Figure 9.2).

Many companies pursue BMI as a defensive move to protect a dying core business or defend against aggressive competitors. But we are convinced that

TSR premium over industry peers, median performance[1] (%)

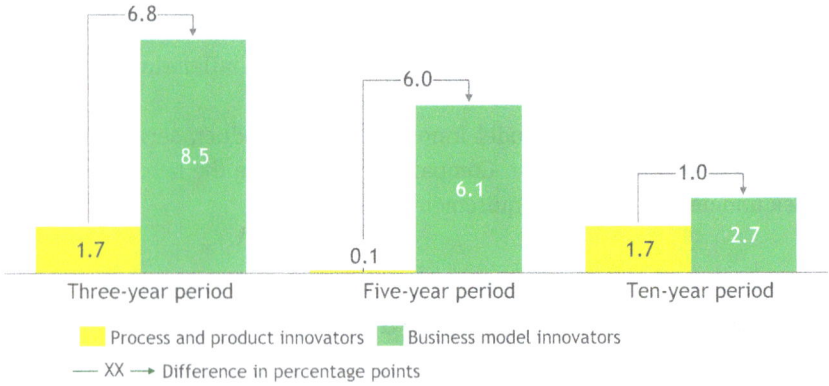

Figure 9.2: Business model innovators outperformed product and process innovators over time.

BMI can be most powerful when it is approached proactively to explore new avenues of growth.

Game-Changing Moves

How a company goes about developing a new business model will depend on its industry and circumstances. Consider the different contexts in which BMI has played a decisive role in a company's success.

Beating Back Intense Competition

In 2001, the Virgin Group entered the Australian airline market with Virgin Blue, an airline that offered low fares with a "premium coach" experience and a fresh brand. The new entrant quickly gained a 30 percent share, severely disrupting the primary incumbent, Qantas. Given its cost structure, Qantas realized that it could not compete with Virgin Blue directly, so it set up a new low-cost business model. Rather than simply copying Virgin Blue's model, Qantas chose to outdo it by creating Jetstar – an ultra-low-cost airline operating as a separate division and designed from the outset to be lower cost than Virgin Blue. Jetstar launched in the first half of 2004, offering new planes and rock-bottom fares. It also boasted the lowest cost structure in the market and has since lowered costs further.

Jetstar's business-model evolution continued when it initiated international service in 2006, making Jetstar the world's first low-cost, long-haul airline. It pioneered a revolutionary pricing approach by offering traditionally bundled services à la carte, enabling consumers to customize the onboard experience with different options for food, comfort, and entertainment. Although Jetstar has replaced Qantas on some leisure routes, its launch has been particularly effective in slowing Virgin Blue's growth plans. Virgin Blue found itself squeezed in a pincer, facing strong competition from Qantas in the leisure and business markets. In 2007, Virgin Blue abandoned its discount positioning and shifted its focus to target business travelers.

Extending a Business Model with Current Customers

JC Decaux is the number-one street-furniture company worldwide. The company earns a large part of its revenues by securing an exclusive agreement for outdoor advertising on desirable public spaces, typically in exchange either for returning a portion of the advertising revenue to the municipality or for covering the capital costs of supplying furniture, such as public toilets. In 2006, JC Decaux's ten-year contract with the city of Paris was up for review. At the city's request, the company offered a compelling new value proposition: JC Decaux would build and maintain the world's largest free (or nearly free) citywide network of bicycles and bicycle racks that residents and tourists alike could use for point-to-point transit.

This system of 20,600 bikes is called Vélib', and it is a high-value asset in a world where urban roads and public transit systems are becoming more and more congested and cities are trying to reduce their carbon footprints. The network is expansive – with stations every 300 meters in the city – so there is always a pick-up and drop-off point nearby. It is also popular: more than 80,000 people use the system every day. Other cities are adopting similar schemes, and researchers at MIT are studying Vélib' to assess the future of urban mobility.

Of course, any new business model requires time to work out the kinks. Vandalism has ended up costing the company more than it expected, and it is trying to claw back some funds from the city, which has been allowed to keep the subscription revenues generated by the system. But the core model remains a success, and JC Decaux is actively seeking to extend it into more cities. This new value proposition, delivered with a new operating model, has enabled JC Decaux to maintain its market leadership. Competitors will also find it difficult to replicate.

Extracting Brand Value by Extending the Business Model

Ikea stores are popular in many parts of the world. But when Ikea entered Russia, the company noticed that whenever it opened a store, the value of nearby real estate increased dramatically. So Ikea decided to explore two business models simultaneously: selling through the stores and capturing the appreciation in real estate values through mall development. Ikea's new division, called Mega Mall, now makes more profit on developing and running malls in Russia than on its traditional, standalone retail business. Ikea is a good example of how a company can leverage its existing assets and capabilities to experiment with new business models.

What Can Go Wrong?

The short answer is plenty. Remember, we're not talking about simple product innovation, but innovating simultaneously – and in a coherent and orchestrated manner – across several elements of a business. Therefore, managers should be on the lookout for common pitfalls, including the following problems:

- *Portfolio Bloat*. This can happen when a company has become bogged down in too many uncoordinated, bottom-up innovations. The result is a bloated, unbalanced, and overlapping portfolio of experiments, none of which has enough resources or support to win the favor of senior management.
- *Failure to Scale Up*. Once a project has been piloted and the initial excitement dies down, a lack of attention and resources can keep it from being scaled up successfully. Sometimes this problem stems from ambiguous pilot results because the right criteria weren't established or the right validations weren't collected and analyzed.
- *Pet Ideas*. Every industry has its zombies – projects that don't go anywhere but refuse to die. Managers find it hard to give up their pet ideas. E-detailing – online interactions between drug reps and physicians – is one example from the pharmaceutical industry of a pet idea. Schemes whose time has come and gone need to be put away, so that more promising ideas can gain traction.
- *Isolated Efforts*. The downside of autonomous skunk-works teams is that they can be too distant from the business to influence or leverage it. Consequently, they may lack the resources to validate ideas and the power or credibility to win the organization's cooperation. Companies should carefully consider the advantages and disadvantages before isolating BMI efforts from the mainstream business.

- *Fixation on Ideation.* Some organizations are able to churn out ideas endlessly but rarely move on to piloting and scaling them up. To assume that creativity is the main or only bottleneck to BMI is to grossly underestimate the task.
- *Internal Focus.* A common problem is near-sighted attention to the organization's internal needs at the expense of the unmet and evolving needs of customers. BMI that takes an inside-out approach frequently results in too little change too late and fails to capture the opportunity.
- *Historical Bias.* Organizations must resist the temptation to overvalue past models and undervalue forward-looking, disruptive ideas. Courageous and visionary leadership is required to overcome this natural and powerful tendency.

Establishing a Capability for Business Model Innovation

Becoming good at BMI is much like developing any other competitive capability: companies assess the opportunities and identify the most promising projects, prepare the organization to pilot the projects and select the best one for scaling up, and then systematize these one-off efforts by building the platforms and skills needed to repeat the successes. Within these steps, however, a few activities are particularly important when striving for BMI.[2]

Uncovering Opportunities

Before looking for new opportunities, it's important to diagnose the current model to understand its limitations. Look closely at each element of the business model and test how the choice aligns with industry trends, evolving customer preferences, and relative advantage or disadvantage over competitors. Bear in mind that valuable insights are often generated by underserved or dissatisfied customers.

Once a company understands its current choices, it is better positioned to brainstorm new opportunities. To give momentum and depth to this exercise, we've found it useful to apply successful BMI patterns from other industries. Figure 9.3 shows three kinds of BMI patterns: innovations to the value proposition,

---

2 For details on BCG's customized approach to developing a superior capability in business model innovation, please contact one of the authors.

to the operating model, and to the business system architecture (that is, how the innovation is integrated into the surrounding business network). This menu is not exhaustive, but it is useful for stimulating ideas when contemplating new business models.

Value proposition	Operating model	Business system architecture
The product as service and outcome *General Electric*	De construction *Li & Fung Limited*	Open *Facebook*
The product as an experience *Apple*	Integration/acceleration of the supply chain *Zara*	Person to person *PayPal*
Trust premium *Whole Foods*	Low cost *Tata Motors*	Adjacency *Ikea's Mega Mall Division*
Free (or nearly free) *Google, Velib' and JC Decaux*	Direct distribution *Nestlé Nespresso*	Serial *Virgin Group*

Source: BCG research

Figure 9.3: Three kinds of BMI patterns.

Implementing the New Model

The winners in BMI aren't necessarily the originators of new models; more often, they're the ones that are the first to successfully roll out ideas that others may have originated. Therefore, scaling up can be the most critical step for BMI. For example, when government regulation allowed generic parts to be sold and thus wiped out the profits of branded engines and parts, GE Aircraft Engines wasn't the first in its industry to conceive of, or even implement, the idea of pay per use. But the company was the first to reinvent many of the elements in the business model that allowed it to be profitable with a pay-per-use value proposition; and GE Aircraft Engines gave the new business model sufficient resources and autonomy to flourish.

An important choice that incumbent companies must make is whether to embed a new business model in the core business or establish it separately. The benefits of common assets, customers, and capabilities argue in favor of integration. But a significant disruption to the current model argues for a separate approach.

The most difficult cases are those in which management comes to realize that a successful business model has become obsolete and the alternatives are in direct opposition to it. The pharmaceutical industry is currently facing such a situation with its intensive personal-selling approach; consequently, it is having to come up with alternatives.[3] In such cases, either very decisive leadership or competing structures are required to resolve the conflict. Successful business model innovators report that "schizophrenic leadership" may be required in the critical transition period when a company must simultaneously defend its historical business model, and embrace and develop what will eventually replace it.

Building the Platform and Skills

The third and final step is to build a platform for systematically managing the BMI process, capabilities, and portfolio of experiments. Most new business models are inherently disruptive and can incur significant internal resistance. BMI requires a distinct set of processes and capabilities to overcome an organization's short-term focus and also to sustain a BMI advantage on a continuous basis.

Questions for Mobilizing the Organization

BMI begins by assessing the company's current context, the needs of its customers, and the models of its competitors. These steps should be completed with sufficient clarity and honesty to reveal what is currently working, what is not, and what might constitute a better value proposition. To that end, we offer the following questions for executives and managers seeking to create a shared awareness of threats and opportunities.

- What compromises does our current business model force customers to make?
- Why are nonusers or defectors dissatisfied with our offering?
- Do we offer customers a better value proposition than that of the competition?
- What alternative models are gaining share at the edges of our industry?
- If we were an industry outsider, what would we do to take advantage of the gaps or weaknesses in our business model?
- Do we have a plan for identifying potential business models, implementing them, and embedding BMI capabilities within the organization?
- What do we need to change in our organization and operations to implement a new business model?

---

3 See Judith Wallenstein, Martin Reeves, and Zhenya Lindgardt, "Waking the Giant: Business Model Innovation in the Drug Industry," *In Vivo*, June 2008.

- What information would we need to make a commitment to a new business model?
- How urgent is the perceived need for change in our organization?
- How should our ideas be championed?

Companies that remain uncertain about the value of BMI should take note: Apple had only one negative quarter of year-to-year growth from June 2003 to December 2015, and it is one of the few technology companies that continued to grow during the global financial crisis. Furthermore, Apple's move into more profitable product segments resulted in a substantial improvement in its margins.

For companies that have yet to achieve the performance they are looking for, there may be no better time than now to launch new business models or transform old ones. Consider the state of your business today. Could you do what Apple and many others have already done? Could you not only change your company's game plan but also change the game itself?

Martin Reeves, George Stalk, and Jussi Lehtinen
Chapter 10
Lessons from Mavericks: Staying Big by Acting Small

In an era in which scale-based leadership is both less durable and less valuable than it once was, many large corporations find themselves looking over their shoulders for the next disruption – the iPhone equivalent that could reshape their industry. In many cases, these disruptions come from *mavericks* – small outlier companies that think and act differently from incumbents.

A group of strategists met in Geneva, Switzerland, to discuss the emerging theory and practice of outlier strategy.[1] The conference featured a "Meet the Mavericks" panel discussion in which four outliers described their experiences in successfully challenging incumbents.

Common to all four companies, the discussion revealed, is that they built a significant and profitable business by *changing the way their industry operates*. Here are some insights on what large companies can and should learn from outliers.

How Outliers Change the Competitive Landscape

Outliers use one or more of the following methods to shake up their industry:
- Focusing on customer dissatisfactions and gaps in the industry's existing offerings
- Being first to deploy a novel technology
- Changing the industry's collaboration model
- Deploying innovative business models
- Leveraging experience and ideas from other industries
- Turning scarcity to advantage
- Being more agile and adaptive than incumbents

---

1 Strategic Management Society Special Conference, "Strategizing Practices from the Outliers: Enabling 'Big Bang' Innovations," Lake Geneva, Switzerland, March 20–23, 2013.

https://doi.org/10.1515/9783110745511-010

Focusing on Customer Dissatisfactions and Gaps in the Industry's Existing Offerings

Founded in 1995, Intuitive Surgical is a surgical-robot manufacturer, with annual revenues exceeding $2 billion. The company's focus has been on providing surgeons with the means to perform complex surgeries through small incisions. By identifying and serving segments in which the value proposition is clear, the company has been able to bring minimally invasive surgery to many patients who would have undergone surgery using more invasive methods.

Being First to Deploy a Novel Technology

This is most common in rapidly developing industries such as medical technology. But it also occurs in more mature industries such as oil exploration, in which small outliers were the first companies to adopt hydraulic-fracturing techniques to access shale gas and oil formations. In many cases, deployment of these kinds of novel technologies requires changes to the business model as well as the business ecosystem – a challenge that incumbents may find hard to embrace.

Changing the Industry's Collaboration Model

Louis Dreyfus Telecom was among the first private telecommunications companies in France. When it entered the market, it lacked the network of the established leader, France Telecom. To spare itself the massive expense of building a new network unilaterally, Louis Dreyfus Telecom installed extra cables and sold the excess capacity to other operators – a novel approach in telecommunications. By so doing, the company was able to build the necessary infrastructure with minimal capital outlay.

Deploying Innovative Business Models

EasyJet, the fourth-largest airline in Europe as of 2013, built its business as a low-cost carrier by pioneering a novel business model and ignoring many of the industry's unwritten rules. EasyJet and other no-frills carriers shook up the business model of the airline industry by moving from a hub-and-spoke model with a diverse fleet to a point-to-point model with lean operations and high-capacity utilization. By removing or charging extra for all noncore elements of the customer experience, EasyJet was able to cut costs while focusing on what customers care about most: flight availability and punctuality.

Leveraging Experience and Ideas from Other Industries

Louis Dreyfus Group had no experience in telecommunications prior to its launch of Louis Dreyfus Telecom. But its experience in such volatile industries as commodities and shipping helped the company recognize the boom-and-bust cycle the telecommunications industry was then undergoing. With this understanding, the company was able to leverage financing and M&A opportunities with exquisite timing.

Turning Scarcity to Advantage

Outliers without the resources of market leaders can turn this lack to their advantage. Particularly in developing markets, many outliers are forced to adjust their products and processes to match both their own limited resources and those of their customers. This "frugal innovation" allows them to do profitable business at lower price points and even to capture market share among cost-conscious customers in developed markets.

Being More Agile and Adaptive than Incumbents

Outliers often place greater emphasis on agility than do established players. QuantumBlack, an analytics consultancy, set out to change the basis of competition in Formula 1 racing. Historically, decisions related to car design and race tactics had been made by grizzled engineers on the basis on their dozens of years of experience on the track. By applying advances in analytics, Quantum-Black enabled F1 teams not only to monitor electronically what was happening on the track but also to play out a large number of scenarios in real time and adapt their strategies accordingly, both during and between races.

Lessons for Incumbents

A study of outliers can provide valuable lessons for incumbents. Many incumbents started out as outliers themselves, of course, but in the process of becoming market leaders specializing in specific opportunities, many lose their exploratory flair.

The first important lesson is that mavericks can help incumbents see the future of their industry. The open-mindedness, flexibility, and faster clock speed of small companies make them showcases of future developments when an industry is at a turning point. When Intuitive Surgical entered the surgical-robotics market, it was a pioneer in its field. Today, for many procedures, such as hysterectomies, robotics-aided surgery is more common than traditional open surgery. Observing models pursued by outliers can help incumbents identify key trends early.

Outliers can also provide a laboratory for novel business models. Because outliers lack the position, scale, and resources of incumbents, they are forced to build business models that are different from existing ones. In many cases, these models have subsequently been adopted by incumbents. Witness, for example, how full-service airlines have copied many of the practices of low-cost carriers such as EasyJet. Outliers can also model a repertoire of novel practices – such as organization models and decision-making processes – that incumbents can observe and adopt.

Observing outliers can also help incumbents identify customer segments or needs that are currently ignored or underserved, as well as the capabilities necessary to address them. The example of QuantumBlack helped other Formula 1 teams understand the importance of data and analytics as sources of competitive advantage.

Incumbents can also use outliers as an outsourced development lab. Whereas established companies can face many challenges in the development of innovative new products, this kind of disruptive innovation is the lifeblood of mavericks. Instead of relying only on internal innovation, incumbents can recognize and imitate new ideas from outliers, as well as identify a stream of attractive acquisition opportunities.

Barriers to Learning from Outliers

Outliers can provide valuable lessons for incumbents. But incumbents, being inclined to dismiss interesting outliers on the basis of their limited scale or scope, do not always hear or heed the lessons.

For effective learning from outliers, incumbents must look beyond the outlier companies' current levels of success and focus on what they are doing and how and why they are doing it. Incumbents often discredit an outlier's practices if its financial track record deteriorates. A shift in circumstances or investor sentiment does not mean that there is nothing to be learned from an outlier's business model, practices, and ideas.

How to Learn from Outliers

Incumbents that aim to learn from outliers can employ a number of approaches.

Look to the Periphery

The history of business is filled with tales of companies that failed to appreciate the threat a newcomer with a new business model or approach posed to their business model. Most successful outliers start by identifying and catering to an underserved market segment (for example, low-end customers seeking inexpensive, no-frills products or services) and then use the foothold they establish to expand into the market's core segments. Incumbents should, therefore, keep their eyes on their industry's periphery.

Conduct a "Maverick Scan"

The mavericks on our discussion panel agreed that the biggest mistake incumbents can make is to underestimate the threat outliers pose. Incumbents should periodically conduct a "maverick scan" to identify companies that could threaten their position and also to understand how mavericks are challenging the industry's core beliefs and assumptions. For an incumbent, this exercise might require suspending deeply held convictions. But it is a necessary precaution to avoid being taken by surprise. It is crucial for incumbents to examine carefully every player that is implicitly betting against their business model.

Ask What You Can Buy, Beg, or Borrow

One of the advantages that incumbents have over mavericks is their superior access to resources. Once an incumbent has identified a potentially threatening outlier, the incumbent has three options: acquiring the company and its competencies (buying), forming a mutually beneficial alliance that combines the outlier's new ideas with the incumbent's strong market position (begging), or copying or adapting the outlier's business-model innovations (borrowing). Which of the three options is best depends on the maverick's source of strength and the two companies' relative balance of power.

Think and Organize Like a Maverick

If there are no outliers in sight, an incumbent can try to preempt a threat by becoming a maverick itself. This requires changing the mindset from that of an incumbent to that of a challenger – developing, for example, a greater willingness to experiment and a greater tolerance for risk.[2] It might also require organizational changes. In many cases, an outlier's business model cannot be replicated by incremental changes to an existing model; rather, it must be adopted as a whole. To facilitate this, an incumbent might need to establish a separate business unit devoted to the new model, similar to the way several established airlines have set up their own low-cost businesses.

For most of the twentieth century, business was dominated by big corporations. Rising turbulence and technological change are changing the balance of power, however, empowering small businesses at the expense of large ones. In the 1970s, fewer than 5 percent of companies that were in their industry's top three in revenues for a given year dropped out of the top three the following year; in the first decade of this century, more than 10 percent of companies in their industry's top three dropped out of the top three the next year, with 40 percent of those companies dropping out of their industry's top-ten positions or going out of business altogether within the next five years. The strong historical connection between profitability and size is also eroding, with the likelihood of an industry's revenue leader also having the industry's highest margins declining from 31 percent in 1979 to just 6 percent in 2011.

To thrive in today's environment, big companies need to be more paranoid. They must keep their eyes open for outliers and react rapidly once they identify a potential threat. But big companies should also act to preempt threats by *thinking like mavericks themselves*. In other words, for a big company to remain big, it may have to act small.

---

2 See " Adaptive Advantage," BCG Perspectives, January 2010, for a fuller discussion of the strategies and capabilities businesses must develop or deploy for success in today's increasingly turbulent environment, https://www.bcg.com/publications/2010/strategy-business-unit-adaptive-advantage.

Martin Reeves, Simon Levin, and Kevin Whitaker

Chapter 11
Leaping Before the Platform Burns: The Increasing Necessity of Preemptive Innovation

The Roman philosopher Seneca famously noted that institutions flourish slowly but fail rapidly. The same maxim applies to businesses. Take, for instance, Kodak, which was more than a century old when it was near its all-time sales peak in 2005; just six years later, it filed for bankruptcy.

How can companies today, faced with the growing threat of competitive disruption, avoid such catastrophic failure? Forward-looking leaders must avoid being deceived by traditional performance metrics and create new growth options before the path to collapse is unavoidable. Research in other fields, including biology and computer science, offers valuable lessons on when and how a business should innovate in order to maximize its chance of survival.

Why do Systems Fail Fast?

Businesses, like biological ecosystems, are complex adaptive systems.[1] Many thriving systems are based on positive feedback loops that propel growth. In nature, these may take the form of mutualistic relationships, in which species benefit from one another – for example, bees collect nectar and pollen from plants for sustenance, pollinating the plants, creating more food sources to allow further growth in the bee population, and so forth. Similarly, in business, a desirable new product creates consumer demand, which drives sales, permitting further product entries and investment to grow the market, and so on.

However, systems also face countervailing forces – negative feedback loops – that limit growth. In biological systems, growth may be constrained by the depletion of food or other necessary resources. In business, success may encourage imitators that saturate the market and commodify the product, or disruptors with superior offerings that can rapidly undermine an incumbent's business. Further,

---

1 https://www.bcg.com/publications/2017/think-biologically-messy-management-for-complex-world

https://doi.org/10.1515/9783110745511-011

high production levels may cause negative environmental effects or other externalities, eventually precipitating a backlash from regulators or consumers.

Traditional business metrics and strategies tend to reinforce these negative feedback effects. Firms mostly measure themselves by backward-looking metrics like sales and profits, which are lagging indicators of sustainability. And once a successful business model has been developed, companies often become "financialized," seeking primarily to maximize efficiency and value extraction from core offerings. From this perspective, marginal investments in innovation may seem too risky. Cutting investment, however, reduces the diversity of the company's growth options, thus creating systemic risk that may be triggered by shifts in demand or competition.

The modeling of complex systems, such as businesses, indicates that for a wide range of plausible parameters, the decline can be much faster than the rise.[2] Furthermore, the dynamics that lead to destruction begin even before sales or profits have peaked. Business leaders must therefore act preemptively – they must invest in innovation even while the existing model is still lucrative.

Companies are Failing Faster

As most leaders know, the ramp-up speed of new businesses is accelerating in the digital age. Whereas it took Walmart 18 years to reach $1 billion in revenue (the fastest ramp-up in history at the time), it took Facebook only six years and Pokémon Go only seven months. This is a consequence of the low asset intensity and inherent agility of increasingly prevalent digital business models.

What is less often discussed, however, is that firms are also *falling* more rapidly. Our analysis shows that only 44% of today's industry leaders have held their position for at least five years, down from 77% a half-century ago.[3] This is a consequence of the same acceleration of competitive threats, compounded by the increased transparency of offerings that digitization enables.

Thus, preemptive innovation is now more important than ever for incumbent companies. How can leaders effectively pursue such a strategy?

---

2 https://cassandralegacy.blogspot.com/2011/08/seneca-effect-origins-of-collapse.html
3 Based on industry leader by operating income in 69 industries.

Lessons from Biological Systems

Biological organisms have been competing in complex systems for billions of years and have evolved strategies that enhance long-term success in a continual game against nature, and against others. Their actions reveal useful hints for business leaders on when and how to pursue new options:

– **Anticipate exhaustion.** Many animal species forage in "patchy" environments, where they must continually decide whether to keep feeding from the current patch – gradually exhausting its resources – or search for a new one.[4] The marginal value theorem (MVT) explains why it is optimal for animals to begin searching well before they exhaust their current patch, and several empirical studies show that species such as birds and monkeys actually follow this rule (Figure 11.1). This would be a good strategy even in the absence of competition, but competition increases the need to find new patches before others do.

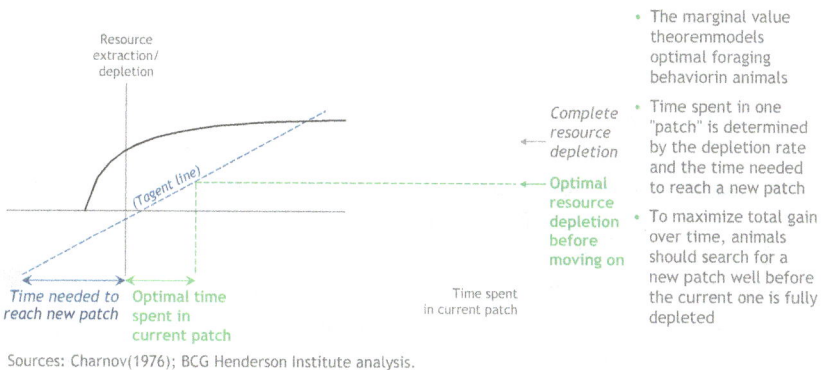

Figure 11.1: The marginal value theorem.

Unlike foraging animals, business leaders don't face a binary choice between exploitation and searching – they can devote resources to both in parallel. But the MVT shows that companies should make sufficient investments in innovation well before their current growth engine is exhausted.

4 https://www.sciencedaily.com/releases/2011/06/110606152210.htm

– **Mix big and small steps.** Biological species provide hints not only on *when* to explore but also *how* to explore efficiently. For example, bees search for flowers in a manner comprising many small steps and occasional very large steps, known as a Lévy flight,[5] to reduce their dependence on any single region (Figure 11.2). This "long-tailed" step distribution can yield optimal search results – especially when the value of patches is uncertain, because animals can use the information gathered from each patch to better understand the environment.

Source: BCG Henderson Institute simulation.

Figure 11.2: A Lévy flight.

In business, innovation efforts should not be limited to either "big steps" or "small steps." Instead, firms should leverage both in tandem – big steps to move to uncharted terrain and small steps to uncover adjacent options at low cost – and learn from previous attempts to identify new opportunities.

– **Embrace evolution.** Over long time scales, biological organisms adapt to changing environments through natural selection. This process requires creating variation in the genetic code, such as through sexual reproduction, which recombines viable genes in a modular way. Even bacteria use a form of modular recombination through the horizontal transfer of genetic information that exists outside of chromosomes, on strings of DNA known as plasmids. Furthermore, some species, including most strains of E. coli, experience more frequent mutations under stress[6] to increase their adaptability. (This is in marked contrast to most companies, which tend to decrease their rate of exploration and "stick to their knitting" when subject to financial or competitive pressures.)

---

5 https://www.technologyreview.com/2011/08/09/192482/the-secret-foraging-behavior-of-bees/
6 https://www.wired.com/2014/01/evolution-evolves-under-pressure/

Business leaders should create variation though experimentation and let the market choose winners, especially when the environment is uncertain. For example, Alibaba rotates a portion of its senior leadership through its various business lines each year, not merely to improve the skills of individual leaders but to combine institutional knowledge from different sources – a form of "genetic recombination" that increases variation and accelerates the firm's evolution.[7]

Lessons from Computer Science

The study of algorithms also provides hints on strategies for preemptive innovation. Several types of problems can be solved with heuristics that, while sometimes counterintuitive, demonstrate when and how to pursue innovation.

– **Constantly explore.** A deep-pocketed gambler walks up to a row of slot machines and contemplates which ones to play – an example of the multi-armed bandit problem. Since the payout distributions are unique and unknown, this optimization problem is quite complex. (During World War II, it frustrated scientists so much that some supposedly suggested it be dropped on the enemy, "as the ultimate instrument of intellectual sabotage.")[8] The gambler's natural response might be to focus exclusively on the machine that has had the highest payout so far. However, a superior solution (as measured by the Gittins Index) also considers that playing other machines provides new information about their payouts, which may be valuable in the future. In practice, this strategy balances "exploitation" of the best-known machines with "exploration" of all other options – crucially, never devoting all resources to exploitation alone.

  Much like with slot machines, the true value of potential innovations is uncertain, so it may be tempting to focus on those that promise the biggest short-term payoff. However, to maximize long-run performance, leaders should always preserve some resources to explore alternative offerings, regardless of where their business is in its lifecycle.

– **Search broadly first.** A truck driver needs to deliver packages to 100 different locations using the most efficient route. This so-called traveling salesman problem is another puzzle that has vexed mathematicians for decades. It is an

7 https://hbr.org/2015/06/the-self-tuning-enterprise
8 Brian Christian and Tom Griffiths, *Algorithms to Live By: The Computer Science of Human Decisions*, Henry Holt and Co., 2016.

example of many common problems in which it is not feasible to analyze every option before having to choose one. Several of the best-performing algorithms for such problems – including *tabu search* and *simulated annealing* – search broadly for alternatives at first, rather than settling on local solutions that may not be the best ones. These methods narrow down a specific solution only after assessing a broad range of options.

Similarly, business leaders should start with a wide scope when exploring new innovations and make "big moves" across the space of potential options, refining narrowly with "small moves" only once the best direction is clear.

- **Embrace randomness.** An algorithm is learning how to play Atari games – an example of how AI can be trained to accomplish goals in a complex environment. One class of algorithm that can often solve such problems effectively is known as *evolutionary strategies*. These methods start with initial decision parameters and then inject random variation into the decisions, testing all the resulting options, selecting the best one, and repeating the process. This can result in strategies that are too far-fetched to design using human intuition[9] but actually yield better results.

When making decisions at all levels of the business, leaders should not be afraid to inject some random variation and test the results empirically, rather than relying too much on analysis and intuition to design solutions.

Lessons from Business

Preemptive innovation is a challenge for incumbent firms: short-term investor pressures can discourage investment, and past success tends to entrench the current business model. But some firms have managed not to box themselves into a corner: approximately 10% of large incumbents[10] are still growing at double-digit rates.[11] Here are some of the techniques they employ:

- **Run a portfolio of growth options.** Forward-looking firms manage a balanced portfolio of bets that span various timescales. For example, pharmaceutical companies know that each drug has a finite lifecycle, determined by competition and patent duration. Given the very high costs of drug development, they have developed systematic mechanisms for managing

---

9 https://www.theverge.com/tldr/2018/2/28/17062338/ai-agent-atari-q-bert-cracked-bug-cheat
10 https://www.bcg.com/publications/2018/vital-companies-think-act-thrive
11 Based on five-year growth for US companies with market capitalization greater than $20 billion.

the balance between exploration and exploitation. Innovative firms run multiple bets using a *stage-gate development process*, which minimizes the costs of failure while allowing successes to be amplified and exploited.

- **Acquire the right capabilities.** To create successful innovations continually, incumbents need the right strategic capabilities. While some firms may be able to build those internally, another viable path is to acquire disruptive companies. This requires a different mindset than traditional M&A deals made to increase scale or efficiency. Instead, the goal is to achieve "post merger rejuvenation,"[12] in which the incumbent injects itself with new capabilities and entrepreneurialism to avoid stagnation. For example, Disney's acquisition of Pixar did not merely result in cost synergies or the cross-promotion of movies – it was also a vehicle for self-disruption. Rather than forcing its own practices on Pixar, Disney adopted parts of the acquiree's leadership team and culture, new capabilities that enabled it to compete in new ways.

- **Maintain dynamism and diversity.** Firms that leverage a diversity of ideas are more likely to challenge the existing model and find new sources of growth. Compositional diversity is one factor – our research on more than 1,700 companies in eight regions shows that having a diversity of backgrounds in management is positively correlated with innovation.[13] But successful firms must also have an environment that promotes variety in thought, communication, and the diffusion and competition of ideas. For example, Morningstar Foods has adopted an extreme "no-hierarchy" structure[14] that allows for "a lot of spontaneous innovation and ideas for change [to] come from unusual places" (Chapter 6).

- **Use a balanced set of metrics.** The familiar benchmarks of sales, profits, and growth will not disappear. Nor should they – measuring current performance is still important for business leaders and investors. But these metrics should be complemented with forward-looking measures that aim to assess the firm's vitality, and its capacity for growth and reinvention.[15] Leaders who look only in the rearview mirror might be content with the metrics they see. But, like Kodak and other incumbents, they will miss the warning signs of the cliff that lies ahead.

---

12 https://www.bcg.com/publications/2016/postmerger-rejuvenation
13 https://hbr.org/2018/01/how-and-where-diversity-drives-financial-performance
14 https://hbr.org/2011/12/first-lets-fire-all-the-managers
15 https://www.bcg.com/publications/2018/vital-companies-think-act-thrive

Past performance is a poorer and poorer indicator of future success. In today's highly complex business environment, failure can come faster than ever – so incumbent firms cannot be complacent. To avoid falling off Seneca's cliff, it is crucial that business leaders look forward as well as backward, and invest in new sources of growth before the peak of their current models is imminent.

Martin Reeves, Axel Reinaud, Johann D. Harnoss,
and Rachel Bergman
Chapter 12
Postmerger Integration Rejuvenation

For the first time in forever, You don't have to be afraid, We can work this out together.
−Anna in Disney's Frozen

An Academy award. $1.3 billion in box office revenues. Millions of wide-eyed boys and girls. Disney's *Frozen* is not only the world's most successful animation feature film ever but also the fruit of an ingenious "postmerger rejuvenation." How so? In 2005, Walt Disney was lagging in creative output and commercial traction. It then acquired a small but fast-growing animation studio, Pixar. Rather than absorbing Pixar into the Disney machine, Disney instead used Pixar as a stimulus for self-disruption, learning, and ultimately growth. This required both the confidence to allow some units to remain separate and the ingenuity to recognize where and how to use Pixar's practices to stimulate Disney's growth. Notably, Disney put Pixar's leaders in charge of bringing new glory to its own fledgling animation studio, wholly rejuvenating itself in the process. The result: an annual total shareholder return of 22% and a series of blockbusters culminating in *Frozen*.

The Overlooked Opportunity: Rejuvenation

Large, established companies like Disney don't have it easy. Many are struggling, delivering 3% lower TSR, on average, than their smaller, younger peers. The need to continually grow and create value is hardly news to leaders of established companies. Seeking to expand their businesses but faced with a deficit of organic growth opportunities, many resort to a classic recipe: acquiring and integrating peers to build scale and realize cost synergies. Results vary. As is well known, close to 60% of all deals fail to create value. These lackluster results are often attributed to poor execution of the post-merger integration. This may be so, but we see a bigger underlying problem. Large companies need a better, more nuanced *approach* to PMI.

Let's take a step back to understand why. Past research shows that business environments are changing faster and are more unpredictable than ever. To keep pace with such change, companies must simultaneously exploit existing profitable business models and create future growth by exploring new products,

https://doi.org/10.1515/9783110745511-012

markets, and business models. As companies age and grow, however, we observe that they tend to lose exploratory drive as measured by the percentage of their value attributable to future growth options, or PVGO[1] (Chapter 5).

Aging companies often optimize for a historically successful model of growth and profit. This model typically stresses the standardization of business processes and the alignment of culture, people, and ideas. As a result, aging organizations are often highly efficient at what they do but struggle to do anything new. For such companies, the typical PMI, focused on efficiency, standardization, and simplification, may provide temporary financial relief but fails to improve exploratory drive.

But not all companies age alike. Some age early, some stay young but then age rapidly, and others, such as Walt Disney, seem to stay forever young (Figure 12.1). We call companies that defy or reverse the aging process "corporate rejuvenators." Successful rejuvenators grow faster than their peers, create more value, and are less likely to end up in the corporate graveyard.[2]

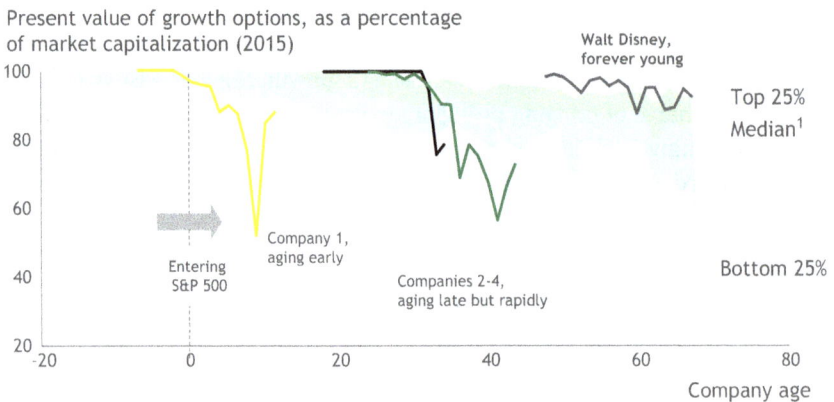

Figure 12.1: Exploratory drive as measured by PVGO.

---

1 PVGO is based on a methodology developed by Han T.J. Smit and Lenos Trigeorgis in *Strategic Investment: Real Options and Games* (Princeton University Press, 2004). PVGO is calculated as the residual from a company's market capitalization and the perpetuity of its current dividend stream (taking into account firm-specific beta, yearly US risk-free rates, and an equity market premium derived from investor surveys) and is expressed as a proportion of the company's market capitalization. We consider PVGO to be a useful proxy for the true extent of exploration activities, but it is by no means an exhaustive measure.

2 https://www.bcg.com/publications/2015/growth-innovation-tomorrow-never-dies-art-of-staying-on-top

Postmerger Rejuvenation

Many roads can lead to successful corporate rejuvenation. Here we focus on the role of M&A, specifically the strategy of acquiring a smaller, faster-growing company to build new capabilities and ultimately stimulate growth. Realizing this requires recasting how we think about the value of M&A. Rather than aiming only to capture scale or growth through cost or revenue synergies, rejuvenators go further. They view the M&A transaction as an opportunity for transformation and also seek to capture *vitality* through self-disruption (Figure 12.2).

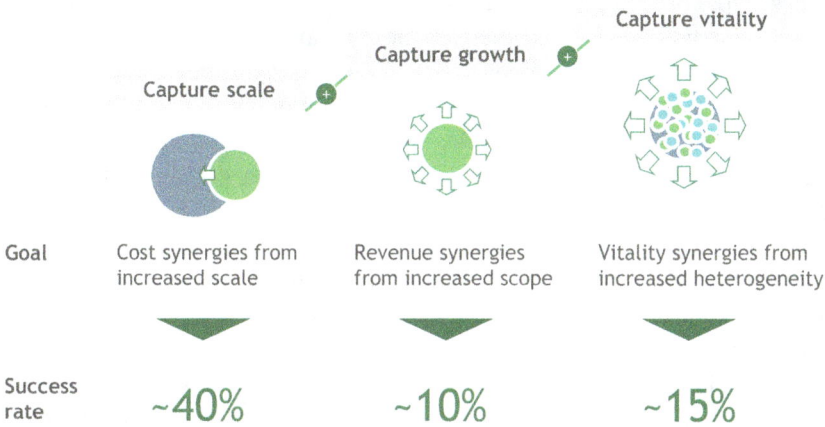

Goal	Cost synergies from increased scale	Revenue synergies from increased scope	Vitality synergies from increased heterogeneity
Success rate	~40%	~10%	~15%

Sources: BCG analysis; BCG Henderson Institute

Figure 12.2: Capturing scale, growth, and vitality synergies after a merger.

It is useful to think of merger benefits in terms of three cascading levels:

1. **Capture scale.** These benefits arise from greater economies of scale in the combined entity and are commonly called "cost synergies." Realizing these synergies requires tight organizational integration as well as swift postmerger execution.

2. **Capture and extend growth.** Do no harm. Large, slow-growing acquirers often impede the growth of a more nimble partner, resulting in the destruction of the combined entity. Realizing growth synergies requires identifying growth opportunities that arise during combination. These can include cross-selling across markets or better price realization. Unlocking these opportunities often requires some initial investment and is frequently overlooked in a purely cost-oriented approach.

3. **Capture vitality.** These synergies are qualitatively different because they follow a strategic rather than an operational or a financial logic. They arise from transferring exploratory practices and culture from the target company to the acquiring company in order to create future growth potential. This can happen via *cross-pollination*, where key exploratory units from each company are deliberately kept separate but primed to learn from one another, or by *reverse integration*, where exploratory capabilities from the acquired company are infused into the acquirer. Reverse integration often starts by identifying, retaining, and deploying entrepreneurial talent from the acquired company.

Are these types of synergies mutually exclusive? No. In fact, they almost always appear in combination. Leaders therefore need to approach their postmerger activities with a de-averaging mindset – targeting the right type of synergies in each part of the business. Balancing the realization of these diverse benefits is the key role of corporate leaders during a postmerger process. In practice, such a balanced approach is rare. Leaders usually focus on getting cost benefits right, with less systematic focus on other synergies. Such thinking reflects the primacy of financial logic over strategy. Faced with capital market pressure to quickly recoup hefty acquisition premiums, corporate leaders focus on the more predictable and faster results flowing from cost benefits. As a result, very few deals even mention revenue synergies as a postmerger target.[3]

Who's doing such rejuvenating deals, and how do they fare? Companies that acquire with the objective to rejuvenate tend to acquire a specific type of target: companies of sufficient size and clout (at least 2.5% of their own market capitalization) with a steeper growth trajectory than their own. Overall, one-third of all deals fall into this category and thus have the potential for rejuvenation. Notable examples for such transformative deals are Publicis with Saatchi & Saatchi in 2000 and pharmacy benefits manager Medco Health Solutions with PolyMedica[4] in 2007.

How do these (potentially) rejuvenating deals fare? We find that most fail, reaching their implicit objective (increasing the percentage of PVGO over three years) less than half of the time (around 45%). Unsurprisingly, companies that need rejuvenation the most – companies that are prematurely aging with low levels of exploration (below the median percentage of PVGO in the years leading up to the deal) – do such deals more often (approximately 35% more likely), but their more exploratory counterparts are significantly more likely to succeed

---

3 https://www.bcg.com/publications/2013/mergers-acquisitions-postmerger-integration-divide-conquer-deals-split-synergies
4 *Harvard Business Review*: "Mergers That Stick," October 2009; Reuters: "Medco to buy Poly-Medica for $1.2 billion," August 2007.

when doing them (about 40% more likely). This suggests that companies benefit from a minimum level of in-house exploratory orientation before embarking on postmerger rejuvenation (PMR).

Let's return to a prime example of postmerger rejuvenation: Walt Disney and Pixar.

Disney and Pixar: Winning an Oscar for Postmerger Rejuvenation

Walt Disney is the epitome of a creative organization, with a legacy of renowned movies such as *The Little Mermaid* and *The Lion King*. But by 2005, the company faced doubts about its creative future following years of poor performance: annual TSR of −3% over the previous five years and sluggish progress in 2D and 3D computer-animated feature films, resulting in a write-down of $98 million for 2002's *Treasure Planet*. Meanwhile, competitors Pixar and Dreamworks released computer-animated, genre-shaping icons such as *Monsters, Inc.* and *Shrek*.

Fast-forward to 2006. Disney, under new CEO Bob Iger, embarked on a turnaround through the acquisition of Pixar. Led by Steve Jobs and creative mind John Lasseter, Pixar had had a string of computer-animated successes, including *Monster's, Inc.*, *Finding Nemo*, and *The Incredibles*. When Disney purchased Pixar for $7.4 billion, many on Wall Street were skeptical, publishing such reports as "Why Disney Shouldn't Buy Pixar"[5] and worrying about cultural differences and the risk of paying billions of dollars for essentially fickle creative talent.

But Wall Street shouldn't have worried about integration. Iger had no intention of uniformly incorporating Pixar, beginning instead with a novel philosophy: "There is an assumption in the corporate world that you need to integrate swiftly. My philosophy is exactly the opposite. You need to be respectful and patient."[6] And Iger walked the talk.

To secure cost synergies, Iger integrated marketing, distribution, and the lower-value-added parts of production. Iger also convinced Lasseter to outsource some animation to India – a cost-saving initiative that was well established at Disney but initially vehemently opposed by Pixar teams. To reap substantial revenue synergies, Pixar selectively adopted Disney's practices of creating profitable sequels and direct-to-DVD films. Disney also prominently featured Pixar characters in theme parks and merchandising.

---

5 "Why Disney Shouldn't Buy Pixar," J.P. Morgan Securities Inc., January 23, 2006.
6 Quoted in "Disney and Pixar: The Power of the Prenup," *New York Times*, June 1, 2008.

Most remarkable, however, was Disney's approach to vitality synergies. Iger began with reverse integration, putting Pixar's creative leaders in charge to revive the struggling Disney animation team, noting, "If you are acquiring expertise, then dispatch your newly purchased experts into other parts of the company and let them stretch their muscles."[7] To maintain the strength of Pixar's more exploratory units and creative spirit, Iger practiced cross-pollination by making space for nonalignment between the two firms. The two animation studios remained separate, and leaders developed a "do not change list" to protect key parts of Pixar's culture. As a result, Pixar's creative talent felt secure as they retained visible markers of Pixar's identity: e-mail addresses, logos, employment contracts, and benefits. In short, Disney approached the postmerger period with a rejuvenating intent and made very specific decisions to secure all three types of synergies.

Fast-forward again – to 2016. The Disney-Pixar acquisition has endured and performed well above Wall Street's expectations, with an annualized TSR of 22% since 2006. The company's level of exploration remains unusually high compared with other companies of its age. In effect, the Disney-Pixar deal set the stage for Anna's promise in *Frozen*: "We can work this out together." And so they did.

Going from Postmerger Integration to Rejuvenation

Disney and Pixar have shown that executing a postmerger rejuvenation requires rethinking much conventional wisdom around classical PMI. PMR differs from PMI strategy in both strategic objectives and execution on a number of key dimensions.

PMR has a different spirit and objective than does PMI. The objective of a typical PMI is to simplify the operations of the combined entity and extract cost synergies. This requires speed and discipline in integration. A PMR – in contrast – is intended to build the organization's capacity for exploration. This requires a process focused on building the machine rather than streamlining it. Instead of *What can we integrate and streamline?* the question becomes *What levers can we use to rejuvenate?* As a result, a typical PMI would seek to reduce variance and heterogeneity, whereas a PMR would selectively build and amplify them. Different cultures across companies are seen as a rejuvenation opportunity, and cultural variation within a company is a necessity for realizing that opportunity. Disney's capacity to see Pixar's apparent cultural incompatibility as an opportunity – rather than a risk – exemplifies this reasoning.

---

7 Ibid.

PMR also takes a different approach to execution. A typical PMI is implemented uniformly, whereas a PMR is executed according to the needs and character of each part of the business. Leaders first define an aspiration level for cost, revenue, and vitality synergies. Next, they build a detailed understanding of the companies and their mix of exploratory and exploitative activities. Finally, they make nuanced decisions on the integration approach – which activities to integrate and in which direction, and which not to integrate and use instead for reverse integration or cross-pollination. Figure 12.3 lays out the logic for PMR.

- Jointly exploiting activities, often in supporting, non-market-facing functions, should be swiftly integrated to yield cost synergies (see the lower-left quadrant in Figure 12.3) This is the dominant approach taken in typical PMIs and remains valid in these circumstances.

- An activity that is highly exploratory at the target company but not so at the acquiring company would fall into the upper-left quadrant of the PMR matrix. Here, reverse integration, meaning the transplantation of target company practices or business units, would be advisable. In the inverse case, the team would typically integrate the less exploratory part of the target to retain the exploratory practices of the acquirer (lower-right quadrant).

- The last case is one in which both companies pursue exploratory practices, most typically but not confined to product development, R&D, or parts of the commercial organization (the upper-right quadrant). In this situation, deliberate nonintegration and cross-pollination are likely to be the vitality-maximizing choice.

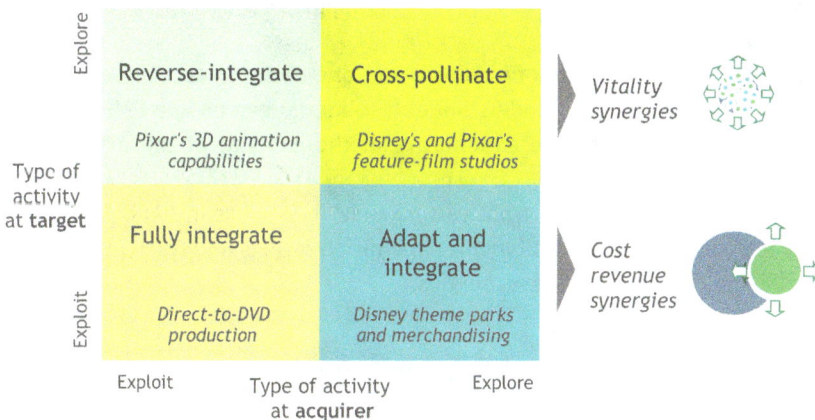

Source: BCG Henderson Institute analysis

Figure 12.3: A PMR is executed according to the needs and character of each part of the business.

A nuanced postmerger approach protects exploration activities by making the company more heterogeneous, setting in motion a virtuous cycle. Put simply, a more diverse company[8] is more likely to attract a more diverse and capable set of people, who, in turn, are more likely to apply their problem-solving skills more creatively. Pixar's do-not-change list is an example of structures set up to protect this diversity.

Reprogramming Your Postmerger Mindset

The secret to successful PMR is balancing integration with deliberate nonintegration, reverse integration, and cross-pollination in different parts of the business. To do so, leaders need to question and rethink five common and apparently reasonable PMI assumptions.

- **Winning the merger.** Companies often equate acquisition with winning and feel uncomfortable promoting a target company's leaders or methods over their own. PMR requires full identification and leverage of the entrepreneurial activities in the target.
- **Keeping it simple.** To stay in control of an impending integration, companies often reach for simplicity. But "streamline, integrate, standardize" is the wrong approach for exploratory activities, and different parts of the organization will require different approaches. Avoid the temptation to oversimplify.
- **Keeping it real.** The temptation to focus on the more tangible and easily obtained benefits of cost synergies at the expense of growth and vitality can destroy value and even exacerbate the long-term prospects of corporations. Avoid such trade-offs.
- **One company.** Stressing one culture and one entity to accelerate integration and collaboration is understandable – but dangerous in a PMR, since it effectively strengthens the exploitative at the expense of the exploratory potential.
- **Tried and true.** "Measure what you manage" still holds in PMR. Hence define and, if possible, quantify your exploration targets and track progress in parallel to cost and revenue synergies.

---

8 "Groups of diverse problem solvers can outperform groups of high-ability problem solvers," Lu Hong and Scott E. Page, *Proceedings of the National Academy of Sciences* Online, September 17, 2004, https://www.pnas.org/.

Large established companies often struggle to keep exploring. Those that fail to do so see lower long-term growth and value creation. To counter this tendency, companies need to rejuvenate themselves. Leaders faced with this situation can repurpose a classical approach – M&A and PMI – and use it as a catalyst to get back on a higher-growth trajectory, aiming for vitalization benefits in addition to the classical cost and revenue synergies.

Companies like Walt Disney show the way. Yet in practice, such successes are rare. We think this signals opportunity. Overall, the payoff is huge. Beside higher value creation, there is something more fundamental: longevity and survival. In 2004, Disney barely survived a hostile takeover bid. These fears have since subsided, as Disney has rebuilt its creative foundation. Leaders striving to shape the future of their companies should follow Disney's example.

Martin Reeves, Chris Barrett, Salman Bham,
and Ask Nørgaard Heje

Chapter 13
Walking the Tightrope: Successfully Integrating while Transforming

In response to the structural shifts in the business environment caused by COVID-19, many companies will need to launch large-scale change programs. Evidence suggests that many such programs are already underway: S&P 500 companies spent 64% more on transformation in Q2 2020 than they had the prior year.[1] Additionally, some firms have struggled to remain competitive through the crisis, creating attractive new M&A opportunities for potential buyers. A recent BCG survey suggests that 71% of investors believe healthy companies should actively pursue acquisitions.[2]

The combination of these trends means that many businesses will be conducting a major transformation and a postmerger integration at the same time. Though this challenge has been accelerated by the COVID-19 crisis, it will likely outlast it – as organizational change becomes an ongoing priority,[3] acquisitions and integrations are more likely to take place against the backdrop of a transformation program, especially during periods of disruption.

Companies that transform and do M&A at the same time, and do it well, can create significant value. However, success is hardly guaranteed. In order to attain the full potential of ambitious dual-change programs, leaders should apply a more scientific approach to change management, reflecting empirical evidence of what works and what doesn't.

---

1 Using restructuring costs as a proxy for transformation spending.
2 BCG investor sentiment survey, August 9, 2020.
3 https://www.bcg.com/publications/2019/science-organizational-change

https://doi.org/10.1515/9783110745511-013

Evidence-Based Transformation and Integration

Our earlier evidence-based research[4] on large-scale organizational change analyzed what drove success in transformation[5] and M&A[6] separately in various contexts by examining externally visible signals across hundreds of companies. We found that both types of large-scale programs are individually challenging, with a majority of companies failing to create sustained total shareholder return (TSR) outperformance compared to their industry in the majority of situations. To understand why some succeed, we used regression analysis to identify several success factors – spanning the company's strategic orientation, target selection for acquisitions, and program design for transformations – that point to some starting points for a playbook when combining integration and transformation.

To identify more specific insights for M&As during transformations, we analyzed 625 mergers and acquisitions between 2005 and 2018 that occurred while the acquiring company was conducting a major transformation.[7] We found that success is rare: only 36% of the deals generated a positive TSR outperformance compared with their industry average over a three-year horizon. On average, they were associated with underperformance of –7 percentage points compared with the average TSR generated over the same period by firms within their sector. This is consistent with earlier research[8] – we found that deals during economic downturns (in this case, the global financial crisis) were more likely to succeed, but even then a majority underperformed.

The underperformance likely stems from the fact that mergers taking place during transformations are more complex, with both entities needing to change simultaneously. Even in relatively stable conditions, it is hard enough to integrate an M&A target; it involves understanding the target's products, capabilities, and resources, and minimizing the disruption caused by weaving them into the existing structure. When the acquirer's operating model is in flux, the integration complexity is compounded. At its worst, the complexity can derail both change initiatives.

For the companies that do succeed, however, the reward is high: outperformers in such situations exceeded their sector average TSR by 11 percentage

---

4 https://sloanreview.mit.edu/article/the-truth-about-corporate-transformation/
5 https://www.bcg.com/publications/2020/transforming-for-growth
6 https://sloanreview.mit.edu/article/beat-the-odds-in-ma-turnarounds/
7 Transformations were identified as restructuring spending greater than 0.5% of revenue, in line with our previous research.
8 https://www.bcg.com/publications/2019/mergers-and-acquisitions-report-shows-downturns-are-a-better-time-for-deal-hunting

points annually. To improve the outcomes of mergers amid transformation, leaders must therefore look beyond the anecdotes, personal experience, and common practices that often shape change management beliefs. From the evidence-based change literature, as well as our analysis of companies undertaking PMIs and transformations simultaneously, we see that the outperforming companies do three things to capture the full potential of their integrations while transforming: (1) they pursue long-term strategic value as rigorously as they do short-term opportunities, (2) they invest heavily in the success of the integration, and (3) they put culture high on the agenda.

Take a Long-Term Approach to Strategy

It might be tempting for leaders who are juggling an integration and a transformation to focus on short-term priorities. After all, both postmerger integrations and transformations are complicated processes that involve lots of granular operational decisions, which inevitably means a lot of urgent issues that demand attention. However, our earlier research shows that firms that take a long-term perspective tend to be better at both M&A and transformation processes, considered separately. These firms don't lose themselves in the details of their day-to-day operations; instead, they make sure that their short-term objectives align with their long-term vision. Successful acquirers select M&A targets for the strategic advantage they confer, not simply their potential to unlock short-term cost synergies; they keep their strategic intent in mind while considering operational questions like where to streamline; and they go beyond preserving their target's existing capabilities and invest in technology, talent, and other areas that will drive growth. Similarly, companies that succeed in transformations don't cut corners or over-optimize for short-term gains at the expense of longer-term vitality[9] and resilience.[10]

   To study how this plays out specifically in PMIs during transformation, we used a proprietary machine learning algorithm that scores companies' long-term thinking on the basis of semantic patterns in their annual reports. Companies that scored above average on this measure generated 7 percentage points greater TSR outperformance. This is a large effect, which indicates how important it is to make sure there's a clear long-term rationale in any M&A done during a

---

9 https://www.bcg.com/publications/2019/achieving-vitality-in-turbulent-times
10 https://www.bcg.com/publications/2020/how-to-become-an-all-weather-resilient-company

transformation. Of course, this does not mean that leaders should take a laissez-faire approach regarding short-term execution – it means that companies must always hold the long-term perspective in mind while focusing on short-term execution. That is, leaders need to adopt a multi-timescale perspective on strategy[11] in such situations.

Commit to the Change

A successful transformation can involve redesigning processes, reallocating staff, and even behavior and mindset change. A successful integration usually means grafting the processes and people of one organization onto another. Both are complex tasks individually. Combining them compounds the complexity because the target must meld with an acquirer that is itself changing shape. To improve their chances of successfully combining a PMI and a transformation, leaders must acknowledge the complexity and ensure that their employees have adequate bandwidth to take on the challenge.

One way leaders can improve their odds of a successful integration during a transformation is to ensure they invest in their integration program. To determine whether or not companies did so, we looked for a significant increase in restructuring spending in the year of their acquisition close over the normal restructuring cost fluctuations within their industry. Among the firms in our sample, 28% did not increase their restructuring spending significantly during the year of their acquisition close, and these companies generated 3 percentage points less total shareholder return outperformance (TSRO) than the 72% that did increase spending. Leaders should ensure that they commit the resources needed to their integration efforts, even if they are already spending on transformation.

Another way leaders can improve their PMI/transformation outcomes is by not taking on too many integration initiatives at the same time. In 10% of the PMI/transformations in our study, the acquiring company attempted to close multiple deals simultaneously. These created average TSRO 2 percentage points less than that generated by companies that took on one PMI at a time, perhaps because some of these firms overestimated their capacity for change and hence overstretched their managers.

By committing to a formal integration program, leaders ensure that the initiative stays visible and has top-level support, increasing the likelihood that employees will fully buy in. And before taking on multiple integrations at one time,

---

11 https://www.bcg.com/publications/2020/responding-to-covid-19-on-multiple-timescales

they should make sure that there is a consistent strategic goal being served. Otherwise, a multitude of different initiatives can create conflicting priorities and undermine buy-in for any particular program.[12]

Keep an Eye on Cultural Fit

Our previous research revealed that transformations in companies that pay attention to soft factors are more successful. We also learned that M&A acquirers with a clear corporate purpose create more shareholder value. Cultural fit also matters in integrations that take place during transformations, and if this fit does not exist, it must be created.

Culture is usually assessed through surveys, but this data is not readily available for outside-in analyses. In its place we use target and acquirer ESG (environmental, social, and governance) score similarity as a proxy for cultural similarity. ESG scores reflect a firm's commitment to stakeholder value rather than just shareholder value. Consequently, firms with similar ESG scores are likely to have similar value systems and cultures. We found that, during acquirer transformations, M&A that took place between companies with similar ESG scores generated TSRO 3 percentage points higher than when the activity involved firms with different ESG scores. This might be because employees of companies that focus solely on profit at the expense of their broader stakeholders are likely to make different decisions than employees of companies that value employee well-being or serve a broader societal purpose. Differences in culture and values can create missteps, frustrate employees, and increase the number of iterations decision makers must go through before taking an action. These sources of friction can decrease shareholder value.

Leaders should consider culture when assessing potential targets for acquisition. This starts with developing an understanding of their own company's cultural profile. Then they should assess the differences between their culture and that of potential targets. All else being equal, leaders should prefer targets whose cultures are compatible with their own. If an important target has a very different culture, leaders should understand the risks this poses and price these risks into their target valuation. These risks should also be factored into their integration plans – by including, for example, an explicit focus on creating a new shared culture, perhaps via a separate workstream. Although it's difficult to get right, a new shared culture can become a source of strength. If absorbing

---

12 https://www.bcg.com/publications/2020/collective-action-in-a-connected-world

a target diversifies the set of perspectives and opinions held within the acquiring organization without creating decision making friction, it can enhance the acquirer's vitality.

Case Study: Konecranes

Konecranes, a global supplier of industrial and port crane equipment and services, provides a good example of profitable use of the success factors we've outlined. In 2016, Konecranes acquired Material Handling & Port Solutions (MHPS) from its competitor Terex, while undergoing a transformation to strengthen its industrial internet services offering.[13]

Konecranes took a long-term perspective on its acquisition of MHPS. Konecranes was able to cut costs by reducing procurement spending through increased volume, consolidating service locations, and streamlining some corporate functions. However, it never lost sight of the role MHPS could play in supporting its long-term transformation goal of becoming a technological innovation leader and bringing a wider range of products and services to customers around the world. It aligned the Konecranes and MHPS technological standards and platforms to enable future innovation, expanding its global footprint and identifying new avenues of revenue growth.

Konecranes was very committed to the MHPS integration. Between 2016 and 2020 it took on no other M&A and focused instead on creating shareholder value through a well-executed integration that connected tightly to its transformation strategy. Even before Konecranes closed its deal with MHPS, its leaders had drafted a formal integration program with nine major workstreams spanning 350 distinct initiatives.[14]

The integration plan made allowances for any cultural differences between Konecranes and MHPS. Konecranes began with a survey to assess both companies' cultures. This was used to define a joint target culture. Finally, as part of the integration and transformation efforts, an extensive cultural development and communications plan helped move both acquirer and newly acquired target toward the new joint culture.

Since its acquisition of MHPS was announced, Konecranes' share price has increased by 50%. The rise was likely driven by the promising progress reports

13 Konecranes Annual Report 2016 (https://www.konecranes.com/sites/default/files/investor/konecranes_annual_report_2016_1.pdf).
14 https://www.bcg.com/publications/2019/bold-ceos-succeed-mergers-and-acquisitions-turnarounds

given to investors throughout the integration and transformation, and the fact that Konecranes hit or exceeded its performance targets over the transformation period. Leaders contemplating a PMI during a transformation could learn from the Konecranes playbook.

When a company attempts M&A/PMI in the middle of a transformation, it combines two of the most challenging episodes in a business's lifespan. Companies that capture the full potential of their integrations while transforming – by taking a long-term view of strategy, committing to their integration efforts, and keeping an eye on culture[15] – are more likely to unlock the benefits of both initiatives.

---

15 https://www.bcg.com/publications/2016/breaking-the-culture-barrier-in-postmerger-integrations

List of Figures

https://doi.org/10.1515/9783110745511-014

Index

https://doi.org/10.1515/9783110745511-015

www.ingramcontent.com/pod-product-compliance
Lightning Source LLC
Chambersburg PA
CBHW061258220326
41599CB00028B/5691